sixth edition

JUSTICE CRIME and ETHICS

Prepared by *Lana* McDowell
Jennifer Mongold

STUDY GUIDE

 LexisNexis®

 anderson publishing
A member of the LexisNexis Group

Justice, Crime, and Ethics, Sixth Edition
STUDY GUIDE

Copyright © 2005, 2008
> Matthew Bender & Company, Inc., a member of the LexisNexis Group

Phone 877-374-2919
Web Site www.lexisnexis.com/anderson/criminaljustice

LexisNexis and the Knowledge Burst logo are trademarks of Reed Elsevier Properties, Inc.
Anderson Publishing is a registered trademark of Anderson Publishing, a member of the LexisNexis Group

This Study Guide was designed to be used in conjunction with *Justice, Crime, and Ethics*, Sixth Edition © 2008 by Matthew Bender & Company, Inc., a member of the LexisNexis Group (ISBN: 1-59345-513-5).

Photocopying for distribution is prohibited.

Cover design by Tin Box Studio, Inc./Cincinnati, Ohio

EDITOR   Ellen S. Boyne
ACQUISITIONS EDITOR   Michael C. Braswell

Table of Contents

Chapter 1
Ethics, Crime, and Justice:
An Introductory Note to Students

Michael C. Braswell

Key Concepts

ethics
morals
wholesight

Introduction

In a general sense, ethics is the study of right and wrong, good and evil. It is a creative endeavor in which a number of our beliefs and assumptions will be challenged. The study of ethics encompasses a variety of different disciplines that contribute to criminal justice, including law, economics, psychology, sociology, philosophy, and theology. For the purposes of this text, the terms "ethical" and "moral" will be used interchangeably.

Our beliefs and values regarding right and wrong are shaped by our parents and friends, by the communities of which we are a part, and by our own perceptions. The study of ethics involves all aspects of who we are—our minds, hearts, relationships with each other, and the intentions and motives for our actions regarding both our inner and outer environment. Being unethical is not simply committing an evil or wrongful act (commission), it is also a matter of being an indirect accomplice to evil by silently standing by when the evil occurs (omission). Unethical acts have to do with both commission and omission. The study of ethics involves a sense of community that includes our family, neighbors, and even the air we breathe.

Three Contexts for Understanding Justice, Crime, and Ethics

The first context is the *personal* one. When studying others we find ourselves questioning and testing our own personal sense of values and ethics. While our examination of the issues should be objective, it should also be personal.

Another broad context is the *social* one, through which we relate to others in our community, both directly and indirectly. Persons do not commit crimes in isolation. Crimes require circumstances and victims. The social context suggests that we need to better understand the conditions and environments that encourage people to become criminals.

The third context is perhaps the most specific one and centers around the *criminal justice process*. A new law being proposed regarding the punishment of offenders needs to be explored in terms of personal beliefs and in terms of the social context of how it will affect the community.

The Five Goals for Exploring Ethics

The initial goal is to *become more aware and open to moral and ethical issues*. In doing this, we discover there is often a difference between appearances and reality—things are often not what they seem. The broad range of moral issues reminds us that where justice is concerned, our personal values, social consequences, and criminal justice outcomes are often intertwined.

We must also *begin developing critical thinking and analytical skills*. If we do not first ask the right questions, our solutions, no matter how well intended and efficient, simply add to our difficulties. Critical thinking and analytical skills help to distinguish concepts such as justice and liberty from principles such as "the ends do not justify the means." These skills encourage openness and perseverance rather than blind acceptance and obedience based on ignorance.

By developing these skills, we realize our third goal, *becoming more personally responsible*. Before we can become more responsible, we must increase our ability to respond. As we persevere in an open exploration and search for the truth regarding moral and ethical issues, we will feel more empowered and have more hope in the future.

The fourth goal in ethics education is *recognizing how criminal justice is engaged in a process of coercion*. Criminal justice is largely about forcing people to do things they do not want to do. Having the authority to be coercive, and the discretionary nature of such authority, creates the potential for corruption and abuse.

Goal five of our exploration concerns what Parker Palmer refers to as *developing wholesight*. Wholesight creates a vision in which our minds and hearts—our thinking and feeling—work together for the common good as we explore the ethical and moral issues we as individuals and members of a community face.

Chapter 2
Utilitarian and Deontological Approaches to Criminal Justice Ethics

Jeffrey Gold

Key Concepts

categorical imperative	Immanuel Kant
consequentialism	normative ethics
deontology	universalizability
hypothetical imperative	utilitarian calculus
John Stuart Mill	utilitarianism

Introduction

There are some factors that seem to distinguish the moral decisions of criminal justice agents from other professions. First, criminal justice decisions are made on behalf of society as a whole; second, the decisions made are not just incidentally, but are primarily, moral decisions. When the police officer decides to arrest someone, or when a judge gives a suspended sentence, the decisions are primarily moral ones.

It is important that we view issues in criminal justice from the larger framework of ethics and morality. It would be a mistake to assume that criminal justice issues emerge outside of the larger social and ethical context of our culture.

This chapter explores the study of two major philosophical theories in the field of normative ethics: *utilitarianism* and *deontology*. Normative ethics is the study of right and wrong. These two standard ethical theories establish a foundation by which criminal justice issues are examined.

Utilitarianism

Utilitarianism is classified as a consequentialist ethical theory. In other words, we judge the morality of an action in terms of the consequences or results of that action. Cheating, stealing, and murder are all wrong because they produce bad or harmful consequences. Charity and benevolence are good because they produce something beneficial. The morality of an action is determined by the consequences of that action. Actions that are moral produce good consequences; actions that are immoral produce bad consequences. Actions have consequences for many different people. According to John Stuart Mill, the fundamental good that all humans seek is happiness. Mill's view is that all people desire happiness and everything else they desire is either a part of happiness or a means to happiness. Happiness is identified with pleasure according to Mill.

Because utilitarianism holds that we should produce happiness or pleasure, whose happiness or pleasure should be considered? The utilitarians' answer to this is that we should consider all parties influenced by the action, and calculate the pain and pleasure of everyone who is affected. The greatest good for the greatest number creates the context for community. The proportionality of pain and pleasure must be judged in this context.

When calculating the amount of pleasure and pain produced by an action, many factors are relevant. First of all, we must consider the intensity or strength of the pleasure or pain. Then we must consider the duration of the pleasure or pain. In addition, we must consider the long-term consequences of an action. Finally, we must consider the probability or likelihood that our actions will produce the outcomes or consequences we intend.

Deontological Ethics

Some people say that a police officer has a *duty* to issue a ticket regardless of the consequences. This directs us to our second moral theory: *deontological ethics*. Deontology is the study of duty. Deontologists argue that human beings sometimes have a duty to perform certain actions regardless of the consequences. Police officers have a duty to issue tickets even when it does not produce the greatest good for the greatest number.

Perhaps the most famous deontologist is Immanuel Kant. Kant believed that the consequentialist theory missed something crucial to ethics by neglecting the concept of duty as well as a more basic morality, a good will or the intention to do what is right. In other words, the key to morality is human will or intention, not consequences. However, Kant draws a distinction between actions that are merely in accordance with duty and actions that are taken for the sake of duty. He holds that only those actions that are taken for the sake of duty have moral worth.

Kant calls the fundamental principle of morality "the categorical imperative." It tells us what we ought to do. The categorical imperative is unhypothetical, no "ifs" whatsoever. Just do it! You ought to behave morally, period. The categorical imperative commands absolutely and unconditionally.

What is the categorical imperative? We will focus on two formulations. The first focuses on a basic concept of ethics called "universalizability"—that for my action to be morally justified, I must be able to see that anyone in relatively similar circumstances would act the same way. Morality involves fairness or equality—a willingness to treat everyone the same way. Kant's idea is that you should do only what you are willing to permit anyone else to do.

The next formulation focuses on the fact that human beings have intrinsic value (that is, value in and of themselves). Human beings should always be treated with reverence, and never treated as mere things.

To summarize, let us contrast deontological ethics with utilitarianism ethics. Utilitarianism is a consequentialist moral theory. We must weigh the positive results of our actions against the negative results in deciding what to do. Deontology is the study of duty. The deontologist believes the key to morality is human will or intention, not consequences. This chapter attempts to explain how the two theories approach ethical issues in criminal justice.

Justice and Duty

Treating people as ends and producing the greatest amount of happiness both seem to be credible guides to the moral life. Nonetheless, both theories seem to have trouble with a certain range of cases. Utilitarianism seems to have difficulty with cases of injustice, and deontology seems to have no way to handle cases of conflicting duties. In this section, we attempt to explore the weaker points of both theories and propose an ethic to handle their difficulties.

According to utilitarianism, an action is moral when it produces the greatest amount of happiness for the greatest number of people. A problem arises when the greatest happiness is achieved at the expense of a few. If we were to follow a utilitarian calculus, the suffering of a few—even intense suffering—would be outweighed by the pleasure of a large enough majority. Most of us, though, believe that slavery and oppression are wrong regardless of the amount of pleasure experienced by the oppressing class. It is always wrong to treat someone as a mere means to one's own ends. It is simply unjust to mistreat anyone in order to benefit others.

Deontology also has its problems. Kant speaks extensively of duty. However, he seems to have no way to deal with cases of conflicting duties. Therefore, it appears that Kant's theory is weak where Mill's is strong, and vice versa. The utilitarian calculus gives us a method of determining what to do in cases of conflicting duties. An action ought to be taken in a situation if and only if: (1) doing the action (a) treats as mere means as few people as possible in the situation, and (b) treats as ends as many people as is consistent with (a); and (2) taking the action in the situation brings about as much overall happiness as is consistent with (1). This integrated approach avoids the problem of enslaving a few because such an act would violate (1). It also avoids the problem of conflicting duties because (2) provides a way of deciding what to do when we are faced with a conflict of duties.

Chapter 3
Peacemaking, Justice, and Ethics

Michael C. Braswell & Jeffrey Gold

Key Concepts

> caring
> connectedness
> mindfulness
> peacemaking

Introduction

The evolution of legal and social justice in America often has found itself pulled between the rehabilitation and punishment agendas. Ancient traditions emphasize the value and usefulness of suffering and service, which are often de-emphasized or nonexistent in new-age movements. Peacemaking, as evolved from ancient spiritual and wisdom traditions, has included the possibility of mercy and compassion within the framework of justice. As explained in this chapter, peacemaking has three themes: (1) connectedness, (2) care, and (3) mindfulness.

Connectedness

Philosophers suggest that humans are not simply isolated individuals, but each one of us is integrally "connected" and bonded to other human beings and the environment—an environment that not only includes the outer physical environment but our inner psychological and spiritual environment as well. It has been suggested that everybody and everything in the universe is connected, but most of us just cannot see the "glue." An important aspect of connectedness is looking within, taking personal responsibility, and acting in a more responsible way. Because we are connected to everyone and everything around us, our actions affect those who are connected to us even when we cannot see the connections. In other words, what goes around comes around.

Caring

One might say that professional and academic ethics have been discussed largely in the language of the masculine or the father, in principles and propositions, in terms such as justification, fairness, and justice. The feminine perspective or mother's voice has often been silent. Human caring and the memory of caring and being cared for have not received attention except primarily as outcomes of ethical behavior. The point is that ethical caring is ultimately grounded in natural caring (for example, the natural caring a mother has for her child).

Mindfulness

Mindfulness allows us to experience a more transcendent sense of awareness. Mindfulness allows us to be fully present and aware of what is immediate. It also allows us to become more aware of the larger picture both in terms of needs and possibilities. A strategy or process that can help us become more mindful is meditation. Meditation can help clear the mind and make it stronger. This awareness can become a kind of awakening, encouraging us to make more informed and ethical decisions about the way we conduct our lives.

Conclusion

If we choose to become more peaceful through connectedness, caring, and mindfulness, it should follow that as persons and criminal justice professionals we will act more morally and ethically. For peacemaking to work, we must examine it on the personal level first. Peacemaking offers us a vision of hope grounded in the reality of which we are a part.

Chapter 4
How Police Officers Learn Ethics

Steven J. Ellwanger

Key Concepts

apologia	noble cause
black swans	occupational predisposition
contingencies	sub-culture
instrumental value	terminal value
latent content	values-learned perspective
manifest content	value predisposition

Introduction

Just as other professions have ethical guidelines and considerations, policing as an occupation has its own set of values and value systems. The key distinction in values of law enforcement is in its creation. Learning ethics in policing is not entirely the product of education, socialization, and training. The learning often predates formal education and socialization efforts as a result of individual, social, and historical factors. The process of on-the-job police socialization and culturalization also has an impact.

This chapter attempts to outline the challenges associated with understanding police ethics by identifying and discussing the various frameworks for understanding the sources of police ethics, followed by the identification of several occupational ethics that run the risk of violating legal, organizational, and societal standards.

Values, Value Systems, and Police Ethics

A value as defined by Rokeach is an enduring belief that a specific mode of conduct or end-state of existence is personally or socially preferable. These values can then be organized into a value system, or an enduring organization of beliefs concerning preferable modes of conduct or end-states of existence along a continuum of relative importance. These value systems form the basis for decisionmaking. There are two competing ideas regarding where police ethics come from: learned (value predisposition) versus imported (values learned).

Value Predisposition

The value-predisposition perspective argues that individuals bring with them an identifiable set of broader societal values into the organization. In other words, ethics in police work are the product of values that are imported (or brought from the larger society) into the organization. Some of the value-predispositions that affect police ethics include: conservatism and conformity, the noble cause, efficiency, utilitarianism, and the role of crime fighter.

Police tend to recruit those who are conservative and conformist in nature with a commitment to the "noble cause." The tendency for law enforcement officers to have conservative characteristics is reinforced by the selection process. "Old-fashioned" and middle- class values are sought out during recruitment and hiring through psychological evaluations, physical tests, and background investigations that often have little to do with police work specifically. The noble cause is a moral predisposition by those seeking careers in law enforcement to make the world a safer place in which to live. The utilitarian value system is also evident in this. In this system, ethical police behavior is behavior that leads to the realization of the "greatest good for the greatest number." These predisposed values come from a number of places, including: historical, cultural, economical, and social backgrounds.

Values-Learned Perspective: Socialization and Culturalization

A competing perspective to the source of police values argues that police values are not imported from society at large, but are instead learned on the job. This values-learned perspective argues that police values are learned through the process of socialization and culturalization within a particular police agency. This socialization process seeks to create a "working personality" or "police personality" within the new recruit as they experience distinct occupational phases during their career: choice (the recruit choosing this career), introduction (where the bureaucracy is learned), encounter (during field training), and metamorphosis (where the "rookie" morphs both socially and psychologically into a full-fledged officer). What emerges from the socialization process is a relatively consistent set of values that are continually transmitted and reinforced among the police subculture through the process of culturalization.

The Content of Police Values

There are five key parts of police values: force, time, loyalty, fringe benefits, and justice. *Force*: Use of force should not be viewed as a last resort for controlling a situation. In fact, the use of force is necessary to achieve deterrence, convey group loyalty, and achieve some measure of justice. *Time*: An officer can never respond too quickly to a call for "real" police services, nor can they respond too slowly to a "garbage" call. When not responding to calls for service, an officer's time is their own. *Loyalty*: Don't trust anyone except your fellow officer; not the public, 'brass,' nor the media. Group loyalty provides protection from the real dangers of police work and from a hostile and unsympathetic administration, and serves to provide emotional support for performing a difficult task. *Fringe Benefits*: Police perform a difficult task, one that is dangerous and requires that they deal with society's "social garbage." Given the dangerousness of the occupation and the clientele with which they often interact, police are underpaid. The corollary is that any rewards extended for their service or in appreciation are a form of deserved and appropriate compensation. *Justice*: The legal system is untrustworthy. As a result, justice is sometimes best served on the street based on personal rather than legal considerations.

Moral Career

The moral career, as described by Lawrence Sherman, consists of distinct aspects that threaten to move officers from the pinnacle of positive values that drove their desire to protect persons, property, and constitutional rights in an impartial and exemplary manner, to the adoption of behaviors that are contrary to department, legal, and societal standards. The aspects are: (1) contingencies, (2) moral experiences, (3) apologia, and (4) stages.

Contingencies within the individual's work environment, therefore, can produce opportunities, incentives, and skills that encourage or discourage the assimilation of unethical behaviors. Moral experiences are particular experiences by officers that challenge their existing morality and allow for interpretation of other's morality based on behavior. Apologia is a situationally justified rationalization that reduces the psychological pain and sense of responsibility experienced by those who engage in behaviors that are not congruent with their ethical values and sense of responsibility. The stages aspect explains the "slippery slope" progression of unethical behavior in which seemingly small unethical behaviors turn into more dangerous ones if left unchecked.

Police Ethics and Control, Reform, and Legitimacy

While police misconduct is not a new problem, it is changing due to the new professional era of policing. There is now a focus on abuses of authority and economical misconduct. With the transition to Community-Oriented Policing and Problem-Oriented Policing, administrators face a new set of problems in teaching police ethics. The focus must now rely on more formal education on ethics and "leading by example." As society's view of the role of police officers changes, so must the administration's view of educating recruits on ethical issues.

Chapter 5
The Ethics of Deceptive Interrogation

Jerome H. Skolnick & Richard A. Leo

Key Concepts

fabricated evidence	*Miranda v. Arizona*
Fourteenth Amendment	role playing
interrogation	slippery slope argument
interview	Wickersham Report

Introduction

Investigative and interrogatory lying are justifiable on utilitarian crime control grounds. While physical coercion during the interrogation phase is quite rare in the United States, psychological persuasion and manipulation are used extensively in order to elicit "voluntary" confessions. Admission of guilt by coercion has traditionally involved: (1) denial of food or sleep, (2) threats of harm or punishment, (3) lengthy/incommunicado interrogation, (4) psychological pressure, (5) promises of leniency, and (6) physical force.

The Jurisprudence of Interrogation

The law of confessions is governed by the Fifth, Sixth, and Fourteenth Amendments. Three principles involved in the law of confessions include: (1) the truth-finding rationale (goal of reliability), (2) the substantive due process/fairness rationale (goal of system's integrity), and (3) the deterrence principle (proscribes an offense or lawless police conduct). Implementation of the *Miranda v. Arizona* (1966) decision safeguards the defendant's Fifth Amendment right against compulsion to testify. In light of *Miranda*, police must advise a suspect of the right to remain silent and the right to an attorney. Before a custodial interrogation can legally commence, the suspect must "voluntarily, knowingly, and intelligently" have waived these rights.

Typology of Interrogatory Deception

The following are examples of the types of deception police may carry out at the interrogation:

1. Interrogation versus interview—a tactic used by police to circumvent *Miranda* by turning the custodial interrogation into a noncustodial interview; the suspect is free to leave questioning and acknowledges that he or she is voluntarily answering questions

2. *Miranda* warnings—recite the rights specified by *Miranda* in an unimportant, monotone style to downplay the importance of its contents

3. Misrepresent the nature or seriousness of the offense

4. Role-playing—good cop/bad cop

5. Misrepresenting (downplaying) the moral seriousness of the offenses

6. The use of promises

7. Misrepresentation of identity (of officers)

8. Fabricated evidence
    a. An accomplice has testified against the offender
    b. The physical evidence confirms guilt
    c. Creation of an eyewitness
    d. Stage a line-up
    e. Have suspect take polygraph

The Consequence of Deception

Coercion and deceptive interrogations can lead to false confessions that undermine the concept of due process. Deception on behalf of the police can also lead to greater skepticism and criticism of police officers. It also reduces police effectiveness as controllers of crime.

Independent Exercise

Explain how each of the following court cases was significant to the jurisprudence of interrogation:

Arizona v. Fulminate (1991)
Brown v. Mississippi (1936)
Colorado v. Spring (1987)
Florida v. Cayward (1989)
Frazier v. Cupp (1969)
Illinois v. Perkins (1990)
Miller v. Fenton (1986)
Moran v. Burbine (1986)
People v. Adams (1983)

Chapter 6
Ethical Dilemmas in Police Work

Joycelyn Pollock & Ronald Becker

Key Concepts

discretion	loyalty
duty	police ethics
gratuities	utilitarianism

Introduction

Teaching ethics in criminal justice curricula, especially police ethics, is becoming an important part of the criminal justice program. This brings up the issue of where such ethics be taught—the college classroom or the police academy? However, there is an increasing recognition that both settings are important. Another important issue concerns whether teaching ethics should be conducted in an academy recruit class or as part of in-service training. Again, the answer is perhaps both settings.

John Kleinig suggests that police ethics is particularly relevant because of the number of issues involved such as the discretionary nature of policing, police authority, crisis situations, and peer pressure. The goals of police training typically involve all aspects of how to perform tasks related to the job. Such tasks include communication skills, multicultural understandings, and training in child abuse and the "battered woman's syndrome."

Ethical dilemmas for police officers can be extracted from newspapers, textbooks, and articles. The literature identifies a variety of ethical dilemmas including the following issues: gratuities, corruption, bribery, whistle-blowing and loyalty, undercover tactics, the use of deception, discretion, sleeping, sex, misfeasance, deadly force, and brutality. One might assume that these issues are the most problematic ethical issues in police work because they are the ones primarily addressed in the literature. However, officers themselves may not perceive these issues as the most problematic.

Barker found that officers believed that sleeping on duty and engaging in sex while on duty were the most frequent forms of misconduct, and they were also rated as relatively less serious than other forms of unethical behavior. In the study, police officers ranked offenses from most serious to least serious: drinking on duty, police perjury, sleeping on duty, sex on duty, and brutality.

Each of this chapter's authors taught ethics to police officers. They used ethical dilemmas and problem situations turned in by class participants as the basis for one-half of the course content. First, the instructor defined the term *ethical dilemma* as a situation in which: (1) the officer did now know what was the right choice of action; (2) the course of action that he or she considered right was difficult to do; or (3) what was identified as the wrong course of action was very tempting. The officers in each class were asked to write down a difficult ethical dilemma or problem they had faced. It is not clear whether officers reported ethical dilemmas according to frequency or seriousness or for some other reason.

Another exercise was to have officers write their own code of ethics in an abbreviated and simple manner. Police officers identified five common elements: (1) legality (enforcing and upholding the law); (2) service (protecting and serving the public); (3) honesty and integrity; (4) loyalty; and (5) the golden rule (respect for others). The five elements that officers viewed as important to a code of ethics were also tied to the dilemmas they identified. Legality can be discussed in terms of discretion. Service is relevant to duty issues. Honesty is related to whistle-blowing and loyalty issues as well as temptations to take money from a crime scene or accepting a bribe. Finally, the golden rule is related to incidents in which it is difficult to keep one's temper. These five elements comprise four categories of dilemmas: (1) discretion, (2) duty, (3) honesty, and (4) loyalty.

Discretion

Discretion can be defined as the ability and power to make a choice of one kind or another. All ethical dilemmas involve making choices. Examples of police discretion include whether to arrest, whether to ticket, and what to do when faced with an altercation.

Another category of discretion involves situations in which no clear policy may be apparent, such as in family disputes. Here, the officer may want to do the right thing, but may not be sure what the right thing is. For most officers in such a case, it may not necessarily be a question of doing something wrong but rather of finding the best solution to a difficult problem.

The last problem situation—domestic disputes—is the single most frequent type of instance identified in this category. Typically, boyfriends wanted girlfriends removed, girlfriends wanted boyfriends removed, parents wanted children removed, and spouses wanted spouses removed. Police officers expressed frustration in having to deal with what are essentially difficult, often unsolvable, interpersonal problems.

Duty

Duty involves incidents in which there is a real question concerning what exactly is the duty of the police officer in a certain situation. Duty issues may also involve situations in which the officer knows that the job requires a particular action, but feels that the action is either inconvenient or a waste of time. Some police officers believe that they have a duty or obligation to help the poor and homeless find shelter; other officers see their job as being free from such responsibilities.

The other type of duty dilemma is more straightforward. Here, the officer knows there is a specific duty to perform. An example would be driving by the scene of an accident or avoiding it altogether because it occurs at the end of a shift. Another duty-related issue arose concerning the risk of contracting AIDS due to possible contact with injured suspects or victims. Finally, there were other miscellaneous duty issues, all concerned with the general idea of using regular work hours to conduct personal business.

In discussing duty issues, participants learned that not all police officers view duty in the same way. It is necessary to apply an ethical framework analysis that helps officers understand that while their position may be legal, and justifiable to some extent, it may still be unethical.

Honesty

Under this topic, officers submitted dilemmas involving self-protection or enrichment, honesty versus the need to make an arrest, and bribery. Many officers reported situations in which they were confronted with temptations of money or other goods. While many officers would feel that it was a minor indiscretion at best to keep $20, at some point as the amount of "found" money increased, individual officers perceived keeping it as being unethical.

Another type of dilemma involved officers trying to cover up their own wrongdoing by lying or not coming forward when they committed minor unethical or illegal acts. Police officers also raised the issue of whether to tell the truth and lose (or risk losing) an arrest or whether to misrepresent facts to make an arrest. Bribery is also a form of dishonesty. It can be defined as a reward for doing something illegal or for not doing something that is required, such as taking money in exchange for not issuing a speeding ticket.

Loyalty

In a problem situation involving loyalty, the consideration of "whistle-blowing" forced officers to decide what to do when faced with the wrongdoing of other police officers. Officers' experiences ran the gamut from seeing relatively minor offenses to observing very serious violations. An example would be whether to report a fellow officer who used what was considered excessive force. Covering up for another officer in the 1990s is more risky than ever before because of the possibility of individual civil liability, and it may be that fewer officers are willing to draw the "blue curtain." Of course, reporting a fellow officer because he or she did something wrong about which only the reporting officer knows and telling the truth in an official investigation in order to avoid being disciplined represent very different types of ethical decisionmaking.

Conclusion

Some decisions have little or no ethical rationale supporting them. In addition, some rationales for actions can only be described as primarily self-serving. Officers are seldom forced to present ethical rationales for their decisions. Some do not like the experience. This chapter presents the premise that the best ethics course for police officers is one that is relevant to them. One way to achieve that is to utilize their own dilemmas. Police officers need the tools to identify and resolve their own ethical dilemmas in the course of their work.

Chapter 7
Police Ethics, Legal Proselytism, and the Social Order: Paving the Path to Misconduct

Victor E. Kappeler & Gary W. Potter

Key Concepts

appeals to higher loyalties
collective responsibility
condemnation of the condemners
denial of injury

denial of responsibility
denial of the victim
police use of force
techniques of neutralization

Introduction

Policing is an occupation with many unique features. Police must be versatile. They often must respond to citizens in times of need and tragedy. Police hold positions of public trust and are expected to not take advantage of people in their time of need. However, police also must assist people with non-emergency requests. Police perform many different functions within their communities. Officers are frequently role models. Police are often in contact with children and young adults. They are the gatekeepers of the justice system and symbolize our government. Police also have been entrusted with the power to detain and arrest persons, to search and seize property, and to use force. Because police have the ability to use and misuse force, they represent one of the greatest potential threats to rights and liberties. There is much potential for corruption and abuse in the policing field. In sum, policing's unique features make professional ethics extremely important in this occupation.

The Path to Unethical Conduct

A way of thinking (i.e., worldview), attitudes, and beliefs often precede behavior, action, and conduct. How police view themselves, their careers, and the world around them sets the stage for unethical conduct. Police often stereotype people into roles and see the world in the simple terms of good versus evil. Police may also come to view their work as integral to social cohesion and order. For many officers, policing is not just about what they do, but it becomes who they are.

Legally Permissible but Unethical Conduct

In most police training academies, the law is presented as an unquestionable system of rights and wrongs. The law is not something to be challenged; it is to be mastered as the foundation for action. Law is seen as the equivalent of goodness. However, the law is often written and can be interpreted in ways that give the police sufficient latitude to engage in unethical conduct in their pursuit of different objectives. Due to the ambiguity of the law and the police's situational interpretation of these legal mandates, the law itself contributes to unethical conduct. Some officers may come to believe that masterful police work often involves manipulation and situational application of the law to achieve enforcement objectives.

Socially Situating Unethical Behavior

Police may behave unethically due to their worldview, the way police work is legally and perceptually framed, and the manner in which their actions are socially situated. Police officers draw upon preconstructed frames of reference to excuse, justify, and rationalize a variety of unethical behaviors. Police may use techniques of neutralization to maintain a positive self-image even when they have engaged in misconduct. These coping mechanisms may include denial of responsibility, denial of injury, denial of the victim, condemnation of the condemners, and appeals to higher loyalties.

Collective Responsibility for Unethical Police Conduct

Elements in society may contribute to unethical police conduct as well. The media presents a view of police as holding back a tide of criminality. Politicians always appear pro-police. These factors add to a worldview of police work as good, effective, and successful at any cost.

Chapter 8
Whatever Happened to Atticus Finch?
Lawyers as Legal Advocates and Moral Agents

Joycelyn M. Pollock

Key Concepts

active role	hired gun role
client-centered/friend role	legal advocate
ethics of care	moral agent
ethics of rights	moral dialogues
guru/godfather role	passive role

Introduction

The character Atticus Finch, in the book *To Kill a Mockingbird*, possesses attributes of a "gentleman" lawyer. He is courteous, honest, brave, and intelligent. In contrast to this ideal of an attorney, there is the stereotype of the "ambulance chaser" lawyer who exploits and profits from other's misfortune.

The question is whether attorneys are amoral "hired guns" or professionals who balance their clients' interests against respect for the law and some objective standard of justice. Legal advocates tend to be technicians of the law, and moral agents are inclined to include a personal view of morality regarding his or her activities for the client.

The Lawyer-Client Relationship

Cohen suggests some principles attorneys must follow in order to be considered moral. These are:

1. Treat others as ends in themselves and not as mere means to winning cases.

2. Treat clients and other professional relations who are relatively similar in a similar fashion.

3. Do not deliberately engage in behavior apt to deceive the court as to the truth.

4. Be willing, if necessary, to make reasonable personal sacrifices, of time, money, popularity, and so on, for what you justifiably believe to be a morally good cause.

5. Do not give money to, or accept money from, clients for wrongful purposes or in wrongful amounts.

6. Avoid harming others in the process of representing your client.

7. Be loyal to your client and do not betray his confidence.

8. Make your own moral decisions to the best of your ability and act consistently.

Cohen's position that attorneys should be moral agents and decide independently what is right and wrong has been attacked vociferously. Memory and Rose argue that a lawyer can be effective and morally good by subscribing to the American Bar Associations' Model Rules of Professional Conduct. They suggest if lawyers follow the Model Rules, they never do wrong because the Model Rules prohibit illegal and unethical behaviors. Memory and Rose do not agree with Cohen's idea that lawyers should apply their own definitions of morality in any case where they are being paid to pursue the client's interest. They suggest that morality is "subjective," and would only result in a loss of trust in attorneys and damage the client relationship if attorneys were to pursue their own definitions of justice, rather than the clients' definitions. Both sides seem to agree that attorneys who pursue their client's interests regardless of truth, justice, or who gets hurt, would be unacceptable for either the moral agent (because these actions offend some larger definition of morality) or even the legal advocate (because they violate the Model Rules).

Lawyers can find themselves in situations where they have social and moral obligations to behave in one way, and legal and professional obligations to behave in another. Should they be moral or legal, social or self-interested, communitarian or individualistic, or as some put it, persons or lawyers?

Granfield and Koenig observe that law school ethics classes do not help lawyers answers such questions. In a survey of Harvard graduates they found that many experienced deep personal conflict in representing clients whose tactics or positions they disagreed with. They tended to resolve such conflict by adapting a "role-based morality." Their definition of good became a judgment of their technical competence, and they exchanged being good persons with being good lawyers. Those who could not left the field.

Condlin suggests that lawyers fall into either the hired gun (similar to the legal advocate), the guru/godfather role (in which the lawyer tells the client what should be done), or the client-centered/friend role (in which the client can be persuaded not to engage in unethical or immoral practices). Scheingold implies that lawyers on both sides of the bar have more in common with each other than the client (or victim), so they really are advocates in name only. Defense attorneys and prosecutors share some vision of what is fair, and the system operates to enforce this vision.

Guidance for Lawyers: Model Rules of Professional Conduct

All attorneys are guided by the American Bar Association and their own state bar association. A standing committee on ethical responsibility provides formal and informal written opinions and enforces the Rules. The Rules cover client-lawyer relationships, maintaining the integrity of the profession, courtroom behavior, conflicts of interest, use of the media, and relationships with opposing attorneys. The most common complaint lodged with state bar associations is incompetence or negligence. Very few complaints result in serious sanctions taken against attorneys. Now we will look at a few of the rules.

The first rules is that lawyers *"shall abide by a client's decisions concerning the objectives of representation . . . [and] shall consult with the client as to the means by which they are to be pursued."* This issue becomes extremely relevant in criminal defense cases when clients insist upon courses of action that attorneys feel are self-destructive or not helpful to the defense. Mather implies an attorney's inclination to let the client take the lead in making decisions depends on the type of client. Public defenders have been more likely to lead in a case because of a belief that the client was too "unsophisticated" or ignorant to make good decisions. Corporate attorneys have been more "client-centered" and have been more likely to do the client's bidding, regardless of what they personally thought.

Lawyers also may not *"counsel a client to engage, or assist a client, in conduct that the lawyer knows is criminal or fraudulent . . ."* The attorney-client privilege refers to the client's right to not have the attorney be called to offer testimony over information obtained during the course of representing the client. An exception to this rule prohibits the lawyer from participating in an ongoing crime or fraud. However, it does not allow an attorney to come forward if he or she simply knows of the fraud but his or her services are not being used in furtherance of the activity.

Blakleyn asked whether attorneys, as officers of the court, owe a general duty to the public in cases that are sealed, but that, arguably, the public interest dictates divulging information from the case to a wider audience. An example are clergymen who were sued for sexually molesting children. It is clear that the public's interest would have been served by knowing.

Vogelstein describes psychologist Carol Gilligan's "ethics of care" and "ethics of rights" approach of the legal system. Ethics of care centers on morality as tied to relationships and the understanding of connectedness. Ethics of rights is rule-based and emphasizes legality. Vogelstein implies the ABA should use forceful persuasion via the rules to make sure attorneys act as moral agents following an "ethics of care" toward third parties and the public at large.

Rule 2.1 states that lawyers *"shall exercise independent professional judgment and render candid advice"* and *"a lawyer may refer not only to law but to other considerations such as moral, economic, social and political factors . . ."* Dinnerstein suggests that attorneys rarely engage in "moral dialogues" with their clients. These would be defined in terms of:

1. The moral stakes of the issue—the more serious the issue, the more reason there is to engage in a discussion about a course of action.

2. The debatability of an issue—if it is in a gray area, there may be more reason to allow client latitude in decisionmaking.

3.   The client's capacity to make a moral decision—some clients may not have the intellectual capacity to make reasonable decisions.

4.   The presence of shared values—when the attorney is very different from the client, there may be more room for disagreement.

5.   The nature of a legal relationship—a simple exercise in contract writing may not create the same need for moral discussions as a criminal defense or custody battle.

6.   The lawyer's objectivity or self-interest—the attorney needs to be sure that his or her moral advice isn't influenced by self-interest.

Rule 3.1 states that lawyers *"shall not bring or defend a proceeding, or assert or controvert an issue therein, unless there is a basis in law and fact . . ."* There is a special exception for criminal defense attorneys, who are allowed to defend their clients in a way to "require that every element of the case be established." If the attorney knows the client is guilty, the ethical responsibility of the attorney is to defend the case in a way that challenges every assertion by the prosecution. This Rule sets the criminal defense attorney apart from corporate attorneys. The most obvious dilemma for attorneys representing guilty defendants is a situation in which the defendant wants to commit perjury or have someone commit perjury to help the case. The Rule explains that an attorney must "know" the testimony is false before he or she can ethically refuse to offer it in trial.

Pellicotti describes that attorneys can play either the passive or active role after his or her client commits perjury. The passive role is to ignore the perjured testimony during summation or any arguments. The active role would be to disclose the perjury to the court. The rationale of many defense attorneys is that they do not know anything.

Rule 3.4 implies that an attorney must ethically conduct a zealous advocacy. There is a line to be drawn as to the difference between ethical zeal and over-the-line aggressive lawyering. Some argue that zealous defense is the only ethical approach, while others argue that the lawyer should moderate the client's interests with larger issues of social justice. Etienee found that judges appear to use longer sentences to punish clients whose lawyers employ "zealous defense" strategies. What one attorney would see as ethical advocacy, another sees as inappropriate "strategy" that deserves sanctions. When that other person is also a judge, it is the client who is often punished, not the attorney.

The Prosecutor

Prosecutors are supposed to be advocates for justice. In their zeal to win, many prosecutors have committed actions that violate the ethical rules. They become legal advocates, but instead of pursuing justice, they merely pursue convictions. Areas in which misconduct occurs include false promises; fraud; threats during plea bargaining; ignoring, suppressing, and concealing exculpatory evidence; and misrepresenting evidence to the jury. Prosecutors have also been found to misuse forensic evidence, including suppressing test results that do not match the theory of the case and using testimony of forensic experts who are incompetent or biased. Some prosecutors overstate the findings of forensic experts in summary argument. These are violations of the law and do not fall in the moral agent or legal advocate categories.

Conclusion: Reconciling the Legal Advocate and Moral Agent View

The dilemma between moral agent and legal advocate has no easy answer. In the end, attorneys and their clients must decide for themselves what they feel is the right thing to do. A strong ethical or moral code can help everyone better make those decisions for themselves.

Chapter 9
Prosecutor Misconduct

Richard R.E. Kania and Ardie Dial

Key Concepts

abuse of power
bias
deceitfulness
denial of due process
personal gain
neglect of duties
nolle prosequi

Introduction

Even though United States prosecutors have relatively few complaints brought up against them, when something is revealed, there is large media coverage. Recent events and past problems are best at illustrating these points. These events include: The 2006 "Duke Lacrosse Case," the 2007 "Firing of Federal Prosecutors Case," the 1987 "Trial of Labor Secretary Donovan Case," and *The Thin Blue Line* Case."

Ethical Problems Revealed in Prosecutorial Misconduct

There are seven recurring ethical problems in the criminal justice system. They are: (1).the wrongful pursuit of personal gain, (2) favoritism and bias, (3) the abuse of power, (4) a flawed personal life, (5) deceitfulness, (6) the denial of due process, and (7) a neglect of duties.

Personal Gain. This includes using one's public service position or office for personal enrichment, profit, pleasure, or benefits not specifically authorized by law, the work contract, or the rules.

Favoritism and Bias. It is unethical to use one's office to aid those whom we like and (in the negation) to interfere with those whom we dislike. This includes political and ideological patronage; racial, ethnic, and religious bias (favorable and unfavorable); nepotism and other family favoritism; and overt and covert discrimination (racial, ethnic, sexual, political, etc.).

Abuse of Power. Abuses of power include prosecutors using their offices to place their values, desires, needs, or preferences above those of the public they serve and over the rules and laws they must uphold.

Flawed Personal Life. This includes prohibitions against personal activities outside the workplace that serve to bring discredit upon the public servant and the servant's agency or profession. Examples of this are criminal wrongdoing, financial improprieties, and tax evasion.

Deceitfulness. The public has expectations that our public officials will be honest and forthright with the public on matters involving their work. This include rules against: overt lying, duplicity, loopholing, and evasions; covering up misdeeds; unwarranted secrecy in the conduct of the public business; and fraud, trickery, and hypocrisy.

Denial of Due Process. Due process encompasses the rules for procedural correctness in dealing with all administrative matters, both within the justice system and in all public service bureaucratic activities. Citizens have the right to expect that their cases will be dealt with fairly and in accordance with the rules for such cases.

Neglect of Duties. A public figure who does not fulfill his or her duties is violating a specific social contract counter to the deontological mandate that one do one's duty, and could be violating laws against: malfeasance, nonfeasance, misfeasance, disobeying lawful orders, abuse of discretion, or failing to comply with regulations and standing orders.

Unique Prosecutorial Failings

There are a number of recurring ethical failings that are distinctly associated with the mission and duties of the office of public prosecutor. Defense attorneys and prosecutors have the same ethical standards to abide by, yet they have differences in their ethical obligations. A defense attorney has ethical obligations that include: responsibility to client, confidentiality, and zealousness of defense. Public prosecutors are somewhat different in that they have a responsibility to the public, no confidentiality rights, and should zealously pursue the truth. Considering that special legal processes such as plea bargaining and discretion are in their hands, prosecutors are dealing with a different set of ethical dilemmas than defense attorneys.

Plea Bargaining

A plea bargain is a special offer made by the prosecutor to the defendant for the defendant to plead guilty in exchange for a lessened sentence. In circumstances in which there is little or no likelihood of doubt about the commission of a crime and near certainty about who was responsible, offering or accepting a plea bargain is legitimate and ethical. However, when the prosecutor knows he or she has a weak case, or there is open doubt about the guilt of the accused, ethical red flags should be raised. Trading off efficiency for a wrongful conviction is not ethical.

Exercising Discretion

Discretion is necessary for a number of reasons. Among the most important of these is that (1) there are not enough prosecutors and trial court to hear every known violation of law, (2) not all violations of the law are of true significance to warrant prosecution, and (3) often those victimized by a criminal act are unwilling to support the prosecution of the offender. A prosecutor has to make a judgment on the quality of the evidence in a case and also in the believability of the witnesses available to testify.

Ethical dilemmas can come about with prosecution. In order to ensure that a strong case goes to trial, the prosecutor can nolle prosequi (terminate the prosecution of) a weak case. Prosecutors also have the ability to consolidate or merge charges, or reduce charges from those initially filed. This presents another opportunity for misconduct.

Politics, the Public, and the Media

Political, community, and media influences contribute to potential misconduct. Prosecutors are political figures; in many states, they run for elective office. In the federal service and other states, they are appointed, but even appointees must be politically aware, as the "Firing of Federal Prosecutors" case shows. Highly vocal and influential voices in the community cannot be ignored; catering to their wishes, as in the "Duke Lacrosse Case," can result in unethical and unjust prosecutorial actions. In the Duke Lacrosse Case, the media also helped to sensationalize the story.

Why Misconduct Persists

A certain amount of prosecutorial misconduct can be attributed to error, poor investigative support, unreliable sources and witnesses, and similar weaknesses in the criminal justice system. Bennett Gershman has attempted to answer why prosecutors misbehave. He observed that prosecutors perceive of themselves as "the good guys of the legal system," but prosecutors face pressures to achieve objectives beyond their capacities, producing stress and lending to the temptation to take short cuts around proper due process. He found the following reasons why prosecutors misbehave:

1. Prosecutors will inject inadmissible evidence to influence juries and therefore win their cases, especially if they are presenting weak cases.

2. They know that a strong opening statement, even if very inaccurate, will leave a lasting impression on the jury in their favor.

3. They know that a strong closing argument, even if inaccurately representing the case just presented, will influence the jury.

4. Their "prestige" and "glamour" as official spokespersons for the government and the people and as the "good guys" in the trial will be employed to influence the jury in their favor.

5.   Their unethical conduct "works" because it helps them win cases.

6.   Even when their improprieties in the courtroom are exposed and appealed, the appellate process often finds their misconduct to be protected under the "harmless error rule" of the courts.

7.   Typically, prosecutors are not held personally liable for their acts and generally are immune from civil suits even when malice can be shown.

Guided Study

Understand the significance of the following:

The 2006 Duke Lacrosse Case
The 2007 Firing of Federal Prosecutors
The 1987 Trial of Labor Secretary Donovan
The Thin Blue Line Case
The 1947 Film *Boomerang*

Chapter 10
Criminal Sentencing:
Ethical Issues and the Problems of Reform
Lawrence F. Travis III

Key Concepts

desert

deterrence

disparity

false negative

false positive

incapacitation

paradox of retribution

treatment

truth in sentencing

utilitarianism

Reasons for Punishment

Deterrence is based on a conception of human beings as rational and guided by a pleasure principle. For deterrence to work, two conditions must be met. First, the penalty must be severe, meaning the pain of the punishment exceeds the benefit of the crime. Secondly, the penalty must be imposed. If the criminal is unlikely to be caught and/or punished, the threat of the penalty is not likely to be "real." Deterrence has two levels. General deterrence punishes offender so others will be afraid to commit crimes. Specific deterrence is designed to convince the particular offender not to commit crimes in the future.

Incapacitation is based on the promise of reducing future crime. While deterrence seeks to convince offenders that crime will not pay, incapacitation seeks to limit the offender's ability to commit a new crime. One justification for incapacitation focuses on the fact that during the time an inmate is in prison, the offender is not able to harm society by committing more crimes. The primary problem with incapacitation is humankind's inability to predict who will be offenders of crimes.

Treatment assumes that crime is caused by a variety of reasons, such as poverty, discrimination, or individual pathology. The ultimate goal of treatment is a reduction in future crime. Unlike deterrence and incapacitation, treatment emphasizes the individual offender. Treatment attempts are limited by our ability to design effective programs created for different types of offenders.

Desert is sometimes called retribution. The desert rationale is unique because it does not seek to reduce future crime. Desert is based on the idea that offenders deserve to be punished as a result of committing a crime. Desert requires penalties be imposed on individuals who commit a crime and requires the punishment be proportional to the severity of the crime the offender has committed.

Utilitarianism versus Equity

The four rationales stated above involve the role of social utility in punishment. Utility means benefit, or the "good" expected as a result of punishment. Individuals who support punishment on the basis of the good it will produce emphasize a utilitarian rationale. In contrast, those who support punishment regardless of effects, based on the notion that crime deserves punishment, emphasize equity, or fairness. Mackie invented the term "paradox of retribution" to describe the impossibility of explaining or developing a desert rationale within a reasonable system of moral thought. He suggests that it is not possible to eliminate desert from our moral thinking. Mackie resolves the paradox by stating punishment is essentially a reflex based on emotions. We react to things and people who hurt us by hurting them in return.

It is likely that we punish because punishment seems "right." Just as good deeds should be rewarded, bad ones should be punished. The conception of reward and punishment as earned is the core of the concept of equity. Modified just deserts was produced by von Hirsch and Hanrahan in 1979. Their argument was that desert justifies the imposition of a penalty and sets the outer limits of the punishment. Within these limits, however, utilitarian considerations could be used to allow different penalties to be imposed on offenders convicted of the same offense.

The Practice of Punishment

Punishment is firmly established in our culture and our history. The core dilemma in the act of punishment is attempting to achieve a balance between considerations of equity and desire for utility. The balance shifts over different times and offenders. As human beings, we must still ask the question: Under what circumstances is the state justified in applying how much punishment to individuals? Sentencing involves the fundamental issue of individual interests versus societal needs. The ethical problem exists in our attempt to determine the appropriate balance of the two.

Contemporary Ethical Concerns in Sentencing

Among the most important considerations of contemporary ethical concerns are those dealing with honesty in the sentencing of criminals, the role of prediction in the allocation of criminal penalties, and the problem of discriminatory punishment.

The sentences announced in court are often quite different from the penalties served by convicted offenders. Growing pressure for criminal justice officials to be more honest about sentencing practices led to federal legislation including incentives to promote "truth in sentencing." The goal of the movement is to ensure that violent offenders serve at least 85 percent of the prison terms they receive in court. Several practices lead to mistruths in sentencing. One is the ability for inmates to earn "good time," reducing their sentence by one-third to one-half of their sentence. Discretionary release on parole also affects time served. An inmate sentenced to 10 years might be paroled after serving only three years. Critics suggest that early release of offenders undermines the deterrent effect of the law and fails to provide adequate protection to the public. Critics imply that it is wrong to mislead the public because citizens lose respect for law and question the integrity of the system.

One solution to achieving honesty in sentencing is to keep offenders incarcerated for longer periods of time. The down side is an increase to the prison population and the funds needed to keep up with the growing system. Another solution is to lower court-imposed sentences to terms that are closer to what prisoners typically serve. The problem appears to lessen the seriousness with which the system views crimes. The third solution is to combine the two by increasing the time served by violent offenders while reducing sentences for nonviolent offenders.

Prediction in Punishment

In any attempt to predict "dangerousness" among a population of offenders, two types of errors are possible. An offender who does not pose a risk of future crime may be erroneously predicted to be dangerous (false positive). An offender who actually poses a danger of future crime may be erroneously predicted to be "safe" (false negative).

The problem lies within the false positives being subjected to greater levels of punishment than they need or deserve based on their actual dangerousness. In addition, false negatives are punished less than they need to be based on their actual dangerousness. Both false positives and false negatives are treated unfairly, and both errors place increased burdens on society. A solution may be to impose harsher penalties on all offenders, as if they were all dangerous. This would lead to "fair" punishment in that everyone receives a similar penalty, but it is a very expensive policy.

Discrimination in Sentencing

The purpose of prediction is to discriminate between those offenders who require more punishment and those who can be safely given punishment. The ethical issue is how the predictive system achieves discrimination. The data concerning the characteristics of persons receiving severe sanctions indicates sentencing decisions are disproportionate. The ethically acceptable factors that predict future crime and explain sentence severity are prior record, criminal justice history, and offense seriousness. Because the sentencing decision relies on prior criminal record and criminal justice history, the effects of race, sex, and class may be hidden from those making the punishment decisions.

The "war on drugs" provides an excellent example of definitions of offense seriousness. Offenses involving crack cocaine have been treated more severely than those involving powder cocaine. Racial differences in the use of these drugs resulted in disproportionate sentencing of offenders because black offenders more often received prison terms and longer terms than white offenders. There is a longstanding concern with sentencing "disparity." Disparity is the unequal punishment of legally similar offenders. Over the past quarter century, numerous efforts have been made to reduce disparity by making sentencing more equitable. Sentencing laws in most states and the federal system have changed to include mandatory minimum sentences, sentencing guidelines, and other reforms designed to reduce disparity.

The Problem of Reform

Changes in sentencing face problems associated with the number and variety of officials who make sentencing decisions. In addition, sentencing decisions are closely linked to other aspects of the criminal justice process. Changes in criminal penalties and sentencing have strengthened the hand of prosecutors at plea bargaining, and the more severe penalties may have increased the willingness of defendants to go to trial, complicating the work of the courts. Sentencing also takes place in local courts, and there is variation in punishment across different courts. While guidelines can reduce some variation in sentencing, there remains substantial local variation in punishment.

Changes in sentencing can have serious implications for other aspects of the justice process. "Truth in sentencing" can produce prison crowding that might result in early release of offenders. Determinate sentencing and reducing the amount of credit inmates can earn for good behavior in prison may lead to increased rule violation by prison inmates. Concern about expected sentences can lead prosecutors to pursue probation violation sanctions rather than new convictions. The most frustrating aspect of sentencing reform is that evidence suggests that attempts to reform sentencing practices result in little to no actual changes in sentencing outcomes.

Chapter 11
Crime and Punishment: Punishment Philosophies and Ethical Dilemmas

Laurie A. Gould & Alicia H. Sitren

Key Concepts

deterrence
general deterrence
hedonistic calculus
incapacitation
proportionality

punishment
rehabilitation
retribution
specific deterrence

Introduction

There are many possible definitions for the term *punishment*. Von Hirsch provides one possible definition of punishment as "the infliction by the state of consequences normally considered unpleasant, on a person in response to his having been convicted of a crime." Proportionality between the sanction and the offense is essential in punishment in the United States. This requires that the severity of the sentence be dependent on the seriousness of the crime.

Punishment and Ethics

Three frameworks address the purpose and ethics of punishment. These are utilitarianism, deontology, and peacemaking. Utilitarianism views the purpose of punishment in terms of the end result. Deontology focuses on the intent and not the consequences. The peacemaking perspective argues that our correctional system should change its response to crime from one of violence, through the use of death and prison, and instead move to de-escalate violence through the use of meditation, mediation, spiritual growth, dispute resolutions, and forms of conciliation.

What Are the Purposes of Punishment?

Answers to this question include retribution, incapacitation, rehabilitation, and deterrence. One or more of these penal philosophies has dominated throughout the last two centuries. The application of punishment has been marked by a move away from rehabilitative efforts and toward more punitive incapacitative efforts. Currently, it seems that punishment is acknowledged to be a retributive practice.

Retribution

Retribution suggests that society punishes wrongdoers because they deserve it. When we think of retribution, we often think of an eye for an eye. However, contemporary retribution is far different from this view. While revenge is still fundamental in contemporary retribution, the focus now is on proportionality between the criminal act and the punishment.

Up until the 1970s, the punishment usually fit the criminal, not the crime. Offenders who could demonstrate successful progress toward rehabilitation could be released from supervision by parole authorities. Great disparity resulted from indeterminate sentences. As a result, sentencing reforms were initiated. The reforms created tension between persons who felt the changes were needed and individuals who viewed the reforms as being soft on crime.

The sentencing guidelines offered severe penalties for severe offenders and penalties that were more lenient for lesser offenses. The determinate sentences clearly identify fixed penalties for crimes. Determinant sentencing does allow the consideration of certain circumstances of the crime to act as either aggravating or mitigating factors, so there is some individualization of justice. For instance, a crime might carry a penalty of three to five years, with less serious offenders receiving sanctions at the low end of the spectrum.

Retributivists argue that punishment serves as a means of restoring balance between the offender and society. Retribution forces the justice system to ignore potentially relevant facts, such as the offender was raised in abusive foster homes. Retributive justice leaves little room for the consideration of human needs and focuses on just deserts.

Capital punishment is often justified primarily in terms of retribution and demands that murderers should suffer in approximately the same way the victim suffered. Bryon discusses the "Their Shoes Gambit," which can be defined as, if you had a loved one who was murdered, what type of justice would you demand? Byron argues that vengeance has no place in public policy and should not serve as a justification for the death penalty in the absence of other salient functions of punishment such as deterrence and rehabilitation.

Incapacitation

Supporters of incapacitation point to the value of maintaining custody and control over offenders, while critics suggest that incapacitation is little more than warehousing offenders, making it more likely that they will be unable to succeed in any world outside of prison. A major problem with incapacitation is prediction. Several ethical dilemmas present themselves when we consider the false positives—those individuals who were predicted to offend, but ultimately would not.

An attempt to incapacitate repeat violent offenders was used in 23 states in 1993. The laws were some form of the "three strikes and you're out" law. These laws had minimal impact in most states. In California, the law affected many of the state's systems and the cost implementations were substantial.

Additional problems stem from the application of three-strikes laws. For instance, prosecutors may exercise wide discretion in the charging decisions of offenders. Thus far, research findings have not been able to illustrate a link between three-strikes laws and the reduction and/or prevention of crime. Some studies note that increased preventive efforts, such as education and social programs, may be more effective at reducing crimes rates in the long run.

Rehabilitation

Rehabilitation characterizes offenders as being sick and in need of treatment. The criminal is in need of treatment, reeducation, or reformation. In the 1970s, the Attorney General issued a call for rehabilitation programs to address both the addiction problems suffered by inmates as well as the need for vocational training. For some, rehabilitation is often seen as the opposite of punishment. This is in error because rehabilitation is a form of crime control that attempts to change the offender so that he or she is less likely to re-offend. The primary goal of rehabilitation is to reduce recidivism.

Cullen and Wright suggest that neither liberal "doing for" treatment programs nor conservative "doing to" punishment strategies will offer significant opportunities for offenders to learn and take responsibility for the crimes they committed, nor will they become the law-abiding citizens they need to be. Some of the treatment programs are intensive supervision on the streets, rehabilitative boot camps, well-equipped vocational training programs, use of probation, behavioral control techniques, and "community-based" programs such as intensive counseling and group therapy. Studies are inconclusive on the effects of treatment programs.

Some rehabilitation programs appear to be effective for some types of offenders. Contemporary movements that complement more traditional rehabilitation and social support models are family therapy, restorative justice, and peacemaking initiatives.

Deterrence

Deterrence is a forward-looking punishment philosophy. Deterrence refers to discouraging reoffending by those who have committed crimes, or offending by law-abiding citizens, through the threat and fear of the potential punishment. Deterrence is divided into two major categories—general and specific. General deterrence seeks to use the offender as an example to the rest of society. Some examples of general deterrence strategies include: increasing police activity in certain areas, the use of special police task forces to target specific crimes such as narcotics, and the death penalty. Specific deterrence seeks to influence the future behavior of a particular offender. For example, a drunk driver who pays a large fine and serves time in jail should, in theory, find the punishment unpleasant enough to refrain from driving drunk in the future.

Cesare Beccaria first introduced the philosophy of deterrence, and it was articulated by Jeremy Bentham. The criminal is viewed as a rational actor who has free will. The criminal actor is viewed as weighing the costs and benefits of the criminal act prior to its commission. Bentham termed this the hedonistic calculus and based it on the idea that people seek pleasure over pain.

Deterrence theorists imply three elements are essential in the deterrence of criminal activity—the likelihood of arrest, the likelihood of conviction, and the severity of punishment. There are several problems with the deterrence theory. For example, how does one know what will deter another from committing crime? How do we know for sure that an offender made a rational decision in committing a crime? In some cases, an individual is unable to weigh the costs and benefits associated with a criminal event such as heat of the moment cases.

It is believed by some that the use of the death penalty serves as a deterrent for would-be murderers. Critics of deterrence theory point to a brutalization effect of the death penalty, meaning that murder rates actually increase following an execution. Recent crime statistics reveal that the South has the highest rate of murder in the United States. The South also has the highest execution rate, with 80 percent of all executions taking place in Southern states.

Unintended Consequences of Punishment

Recent statistics indicate that approximately 1.3 million adults are confined in state and federal prisons. This boom in incarceration has lead to overcrowding and a struggle by states to find cost-saving alternatives. One solution is privatization, yet privatization leaves many questions unanswered and has some serious ethical implications.

One of the severe impacts of overcrowding is that conditions of confinement are changed, such as a decline of physical, social, and operational conditions inside prison facilities. Moreover, overcrowding impedes correctional officers' abilities to classify and separate inmates according to treatment, safety, and security needs. State prison inmates suffer form a variety of diseases. Because mass screening programs are currently not in place in most correctional facilities, the data of inmates with STDs is incomplete.

Ethical Dilemmas in Punishment

Privatization of correctional facilities requires that we ask "who should punish"? Should corrections be a money-making enterprise? Should governments delegate coercive authority to private entities?

Full-scale privatization refers to institutions that are privately owned and operated by a corporation. Those who oppose privatization suggest that giving the power over undermines the legitimacy of government. The use of the death penalty poses ethical problems such as "what types of punishments should we utilize?" For some, death is seen as the ultimate punishment for persons found guilty of committing the most heinous crimes. Opponents of the death penalty suggest that it is cruel and unusual punishment. There are also problems with executing innocent people, arbitrary applications, and the execution of juveniles.

The punishment of special populations such as the mentally ill and juvenile offenders present problems as well. An ethical issue arises when one is faced with the quality of life for severely mentally ill inmates. These offenders are more likely to be victimized, be beaten, and commit suicide. The mentally ill represent 16 percent of the prison population.

Treating juvenile offenders as adults is another key ethical concern. Gaarder and Belknap imply that over the past 10 years, there has been a nationwide effort to treat juveniles as adults, mainly with the "get tough" movement. Many scholars agree that sentencing should be different for juvenile offenders due to their lack of mental development necessary to form intent.

Conclusion

The main ethical questions in this paper include those on privatization ("Who should punish, the state or private correctional firms?"), the death penalty ("What types of punishments should we utilize and how severe should they be?"), and special populations ("Should we punish all offenders the same?").

While rehabilitation is still espoused by system officials, it is no longer the primary goal of correctional authorities. In place of rehabilitation, correctional policies are increasingly employing retributive and incapacitative strategies. The overall crime rate has witnessed moderate decreases in the past few years, possibly partially due to the implementation of such strategies. The unintended consequences of incapacitative strategies of overcrowding prisons have increased the violence and the number of health-related problems within the correctional walls.

Chapter 12
To Die or Not to Die:
Morality Ethics, and the Death Penalty

John Whitehead & Michael Braswell

Key Concepts

    arbitrariness
    death penalty
    deterrence
    discrimination
    incapacitation

Introduction

In 2002, 71 individuals were executed in the United States. Fifty-four percent of individuals on death row in 2002 were white and 44 percent were black. Almost 99 percent of individuals were male, and the majority had less than a high school diploma or GED.

Should There Be a Death Penalty?

The death penalty is often argued in terms of religious values and beliefs. Individuals not in favor of the death penalty suggest two wrongs do not make a right while advocates imply that the ultimate crime requires the ultimate punishment. The judicial question of whether the criminal justice process prosecute capital cases justly and equitably is also raised by society. Race, gender, and economic bias are often debated and discussed when attempting to answer this question. Opponents of the death penalty suggest that life without parole sentences are more appropriate because if a mistake is made, the person is still alive. Utilitarians argue that the death penalty has positive consequences which justify its use, such as deterrence and incapacitation.

Deterrence

Deterrence theory maintains that for any punishment or sanction to be an effective deterrent, the penalty in question must be severe, certain, and quick. Problems arise with the death penalty in the areas of certainty and quickness. Utilitarians in favor of the death penalty imply that it is a general deterrent, meaning that others will be less likely to commit crimes. Opponents argue that several problems exist with the deterrence argument. Many individuals who murder may not think about possible penalties. In addition, many murders are spur-of-the-moment crimes. Sellin concluded in his 1980 study that states that have the death penalty do not have lower homicide rates than states without the death penalty. In addition, scientific research studies on the effectiveness of Scared Straight type programs indicate there are no significant differences between youths who experience such a program and youth who do not go to such sessions.

Incapacitation

Executing an offender prevents him or her from ever killing again, so in a way, the death penalty does satisfy the utilitarian goal of incapacitation. Opponents argue that other penalties can also achieve very high degrees of incapacitation. There is substantial evidence that if society punished convicted murderers with 10 to 20 years of imprisonment and then released them on parole, the released murderers would have very low recidivism rates. A few reasons for the success of parolees are that parole boards are careful in making a parole decision in murder cases and inmates usually serve 10 or more years in prison before release. A minority, about 10 percent of parolees, do indeed commit a new felony.

Peacemaking Perspective

The peacemaking perspective opposes the death penalty, arguing that it does not promote caring, connectedness, and mindfulness whereas other penalties do. Jarvis Masters is a death row inmate who has used his time in prison to examine his life and turn from crime and violence to Buddhism and promoting peace. Jarvis a good example of an offender who changed in prison and has had a positive effect on other prisoners. Peacemaking criminologists are also concerned with the effects of death row on the family members of the death row inmates. The peacemaking perspective suggests that sending offenders to death row seems to foster seeing these criminals as outside the human family and permitting the rest of us to depict them as less than human.

Mistakes

Juries and judges make mistakes in determining guilt and in deciding sentences. A major source is the quality of defense representation. Many states provide very modest compensation so it is often difficult to attract qualified individuals to work death penalty cases. The "death belt" is made up of nine Southern states that utilize the death penalty frequently. Another mistake is inaccurate eyewitness testimonies. Proponents of the death penalty suggest that mistakes happen in all walks of life. The question becomes, do you except the death penalty if you or a loved one is the one experiencing the mistake?

Discrimination and Racial Bias

Death row is disproportionately black. African Americans make up approximately 12 percent of the U.S. population and constitute 44 percent of the prisoners on death row. The Capital Jury Project found that the number of white males or even the presence of one black juror on a jury can make a significant difference in the decisions made by juries. It is imperative to eliminate discrimination. Discrimination or the appearance of discrimination can influence minority members to have negative attitudes toward police, judges, and others in the criminal justice system.

Arbitrariness

Approximately 20,000 murders are committed each year in the United States, and fewer than 500 cases result in the death penalty. One problem is black defendant/white victim cases are more likely to result in the death penalty than black defendant/black victim cases. Moreover, location, judge, prosecutor, and notoriety of the case also play a role in determining whether one receives the death penalty. The deontological view would argue that arbitrariness should play no role because the categorical imperative calls for treating similarly situated individuals in a similar fashion. Arbitrariness is hard to eliminate because offenders may be allowed reductions of their sentence for providing information on other criminals. Another effort to reduce arbitrariness is proportionality review, meaning that courts review death penalty cases in the jurisdiction to attempt to ensure only the most horrible murders get the death penalty. The problem with proportionality reviews is that measuring severity is not simple.

Conditions on Death Row

There are two main types of death row: unreformed and reformed. Unreformed death rows involve a great deal of isolation; reformed death rows allow prisoners to spend much more time out of their cells for work and recreation. Robert Johnson argues that a reformed death row does not help a prisoner get ready for his or her own death. Aside from Johnson, though, most inmates, guards, and critics would probably endorse the reformed death row.

Jurors in Capital Cases

Many jurors make the decision in favor of the death penalty too soon. Many jurors also have inaccurate beliefs about how many years a prisoner would have to serve in prison if he received a prison sentence instead of the death penalty. Capital jurors are often confused about mitigating factors that are a critical part of the decision to impose the death penalty. The issue of the impact of race is also considered by the jurors.

Religion and Capital Punishment

Many people use religion to justify their views on the death penalty. Many Christians point to Paul's Letter to the Romans as proof that God endorses the death penalty when used appropriately. Another example is when a woman was brought to Jesus for adultery. The penalty was capital punishment, but Jesus told the questioners that "he who is without sin should case the first stone." Many see this as Jesus' rejection of the death penalty. Societal conditions have changed considerably since the time of Jesus. Prisons and lengthy sentences were simply not a viable alternative to capital punishment at the time of Jesus. Both the Roman Catholic Church and the Presbyterian Church have issued formal statements opposing the death penalty, yet the Southern Baptist Convention has issued a statement in favor of the death penalty.

Chapter 13

Ethical Issues in Probation, Parole, and Community Corrections

John T. Whitehead

Key Concepts

community supervision
parole
probation
whistle-blowing

Introduction

Joan Petersilia of the RAND Corporation authored a report of the effectiveness of probation supervision for felons in California. The report indicated serious problems with felony probation: 65 percent of the felons studied were rearrested within 40 months, and one-third were re-incarcerated. It is not surprising, then, that there is some question as to the effectiveness of community supervision.

There are several frequent observations in response to such negative reports. First, the governmental bodies are unwilling to spend enough money on probation. Second, part of the problem may be due to workers not doing the jobs that they should be doing. Workers may not be living up to the ethical standard of putting in a full day's work for a full day's pay. Third, there is no consensus in criminology as to which forms of rehabilitation work and which do not. Moreover, criminology has yet to provide a unified theory of criminality and offending.

The Mission of Probation and Parole

Traditionally, the mission of probation and parole supervision has been described as some combination of assistance and control, treatment and security, or service and surveillance. The ethical perspective to this mission involves whether offenders are totally free and responsible, and whether society has some obligation to help offenders to some degree. Recent developments in community supervision, such as house arrest, electronic monitoring of offenders, intensive supervision, and calls for the elimination of parole, raise important ethical considerations.

Supervision Fees

Related to the issue of increasing emphasis on surveillance techniques in community supervision is the question of charging probationers and parolees supervision fees. This growing trend in community corrections raises some important ethical considerations. On the one hand, collecting money can detract from the supervision officer's main mission of risk control. Likewise, fees represent a financial burden for many offenders. On the other hand, fees have no negative impact on the collection of restitution orders or the service mission itself. Furthermore, supervision fees are politically attractive.

Ethical Issues in Presentence Investigation

The main ethical issue in presentence investigation appears to be deceptiveness. Officers attempt to establish rapport with defendants during interviews aimed at obtaining information for the reports. The presentence investigation, then, is not really an investigation. Rather, it involves the probation officer's preparation of the defendant for the sentence. Presentence investigation reports provide information useful to probation officers who supervise offenders sentenced to probation. In addition, the reports also convey such information to prison officials for incarcerated defendants. In both instances, important details about the offender's educational background, intelligence, psychological state, work experience, and so forth are available so that correctional officials can plan appropriate intervention strategies. The notion that the presentence report is a hallmark of individualized justice is false.

Whistle-blowing

Making internal complaints outside the department is known as "whistle-blowing." In the context of probation, whistle-blowing involves a five-stage process: (1) internal criticism within a given department of questionable or unethical activity, (2) state of intransigency, (3) external disclosure of unethical activities, (4) organizational reaction, and (5) the aftermath. Probation administrators are often unresponsive to line officers raising ethical questions, and whistle-blowing employees are typically transferred to unimportant assignments.

The Role of the Victim

Victims are involved in several stages of probation and parole. Victims can and should enter into the presentence investigation process. Other related ethical issues involve the idea of restitution. First, we need a reliable and precise way of determining the amount of restitution. Second, we need to decide if factors such as depreciation, market demand, condition, and victim involvement in the crime influence the amount of restitution.

Chapter 14
Restorative Justice
and the Peacemaking Ethic

Lana McDowell, Michael C. Braswell & John T. Whitehead

Key Concepts

family group conferencing
peacemaking
reintegrative shaming
restorative justice
reparative boards

sentencing circles
victim-offender panels
victim-offender reconciliation programs
wisdom traditions

Introduction

While peacemaking theories and restorative justice began to make their way in the 1990s, these principles are closely related to the way that cultures have dealt with crime and punishment internally for many years. When viewing crime and justice in a peacemaking and restorative manner, one understands that punishing the offender is not the only action that may be taken. Focusing on the needs of the victim(s) and the community in the process of justice is important as well. In order to practice these principles, one must possess these peacemaking virtues: self-honesty, courage, kindness, and a sense of humor.

The Four Qualities of Restorative Justice

Quality 1: The ability to reconcile differences of all parties involved.

Quality 2: The ability of the offenders to hold themselves accountable for their actions.

Quality 3: The ability for victims to feel their experiences have been truly heard and recognized, their emotions have been felt, and the harm done to them has been mended.

Quality 4: The ability for the community to actively be involved in the process of justice.

Evolution of Restorative Justice and the Peacemaking Ethic

The traditional view of justice focuses on enforcement of the laws with an eye toward punishment. An individual who commits a crime is said to have acted against the social contract written into statutory law. Professionals in the traditional criminal justice system are charged with carrying out the necessary punishment. Restorative justice and peacemaking criminology take a more proactive approach to crime by helping the offender to more fully understand and take responsibility for the personal harm he or she has caused others. Such an approach can at least increase the odds that the offender will more seriously consider the effects and consequences of his or her future actions.

Peacemaking and the Wisdom Traditions

The roots of the three peacemaking themes—care, connectedness, and mindfulness—are reflected in such ancient-wisdom traditions as Christianity, Judaism, Taoism, Hinduism, Buddhism, Islam, and Native American traditions. The ideas of connectedness, care, and mindfulness are enmeshed within each of the tradition's tenets. Differences may be noted regarding the vast array of religious thought that makes up the wisdom traditions. However, their similarities regarding the themes of peacemaking criminology are the focus of this section.

Core Elements of Restorative Justice

There are a number of values that should be engrained within restorative justice management teams: amends, assistance, collaboration, empowerment, encounter, inclusion, moral education, protection, reintegration, and resolution. There are also three principles of restorative justice:

Principle 1. Justice requires that we work to heal victims, offenders, and communities injured by crime.

Principle 2. Victims, offenders, and communities should have the opportunity for active involvement in the justice process as early and as fully as they wish.

Principle 3. We must rethink the relative roles and responsibilities of government and community: In promoting justice, government is responsible for preserving a just order and the community for establishing a just peace.

Types of Restorative Justice Programs

Family Group Conferencing: The offender, victim, family members, community members, and professionals meet to discuss the wrongdoing and create a plan regarding the most appropriate method of reintegration for both the offender and victim.

Victim-Offender Reconciliation Programs: The victim and offender meet face to face with a mediator present to discuss the transgression at hand.

Sentencing Circles: Community members, the victim, the offender, and court officials each have the ability to speak and jointly create a solution regarding the outcome of the criminal action at hand.

Reparative Boards: A series of public meetings is organized and implemented by community members regarding steps an offender shall take to restore the harm done to the victim(s) and the community.

Victim-Offender Panels: Victims are provided the opportunity to speak with a group of offenders who have been convicted of the crime the victim has suffered without being required to meet their personal assailant.

Reintegrative Shaming: The community expresses its disappointment in the offender regarding his or her criminal actions.

A Precarious Balance

The effects of restorative community justice are uncertain today because evaluations of such programs are in their infancy. The problem lies with the question of how do we measure the effectiveness of restorative justice? Because the goal of restorative justice is not only to prevent crime but also to restore the relationships between the offender, victim, and the community, evaluation is not as simple as checking recidivism rates. The current research conducted regarding the effectiveness of restorative community justice programs leaves us with a mixed understanding. Some studies show only mixed or modest results while others show participants benefiting from the practices.

Conclusion

While restorative justice principles seem to be idealistic and unachievable in today's world, the practices and ideas behind it come from a deeper part of our human understanding.

Chapter 15
Keeping an Eye on the Keeper:
Prison Corruption and Its Control

Bernard J. McCarthy

Key Concepts

corruption
corruption through default
corruption through friendship
corruption through reciprocity
malfeasance
material accommodations

misfeasance
nonfeasance
"pains of imprisonment"
power accommodations
status accommodations

Introduction

This chapter focuses on a troublesome problem in the administration of justice in American prison systems. It involves a personal choice by employees to engage in behavior that is clearly wrong and damaging. Corruption serves to negate the goals and processes of corrections and breeds disrespect for the process and the aims of justice. Prisons are one of the most visible and symbolic aspects of the coercive nature of criminal justice and at the same time one that is most closed to the public. More recently, prisons in American have become more punitive in their outlook and operating philosophy and the conditions of confinement more severe. Supreme Court Justice Kennedy in a speech to the American Bar Association described the prison as "the hidden world of punishment; (and) we would be startled by what we see" if we were to look.

One of the most critical elements in any correctional system is the quality of staff that are hired to work in prisons. Corrupt practices in prison range from simple acts of theft and pilferage to large-scale criminal conspiracies. The impact of such practices cannot be underestimated. The existence of corrupt practices also undermines the impact of correctional programs designed to change offenders. From the offenders' perspective, they have everything to gain to persuade staff to make decisions that benefit them personally and very little to lose. From the employees' perspective, corrupt practices represent a lucrative way to supplement one's income.

In examining staff corruption within a prison system, three basic questions are raised: First, what is corruption, and what forms does it take in a prison setting? Second, what factors appear to be associated with it? Third, what steps should be taken to control the problem?

51

Defining Corruption in a Correctional Environment

Corruption is defined more specifically as the "intentional violation of organizational norms" by employees for personal gain, usually of a material nature. Prison corruption occurs when an employee violates organizational rules and regulations for his or her own personal material gain. Before an action can be deemed corrupt, the action must involve individuals who are employees. In addition, the offense must violate the formal rules of the organization or agency. Lastly, for an action to be corrupt, the offense must involve an employee receiving some specific, personal material gain for his or his misconduct.

Types of Prison Corruption

The review of prison internal affairs case files identified several types of corrupt conduct: theft, trafficking in contraband, embezzlement, misuse of authority, and a residual or miscellaneous category. More recently, dozens of staff and inmates have been arrested across the country for smuggling in cell phones to inmates. These phones have been used to continue outside criminal activities. Misuse of authority is a general category involving the intentional misuse of discretion for personal material gain.

This form of corruption consisted of three basic offenses directed against inmates: the acceptance of gratuities from inmates for special consideration in obtaining legitimate prison privileges; the acceptance of gratuities for special consideration in obtaining or protecting illicit prison activities; and the mistreatment or extortion of inmates by staff for personal material gain. An additional form of misuse of authority is the taking of bribes by correctional administrators to award contracts to private vendors for services needed by the correctional system. Another form of misuse of authority is sexual misconduct involving staff and inmates, staff against staff, and staff and offender family members/friends. One major reason for this upswing in allegations and charges is the use of cross-gender assignments in prisons.

The Role of Discretion

The different types of corruption involve the misuse or abuse of discretion by correctional staff members. The three forms of discretionary misconduct are: (1) misfeasance, (2) malfeasance, and (3) nonfeasance.

Misfeasance refers to the improper performance of some act that an official may lawfully do. Offenses in this area include the acceptance of gratuities for special privileges or preferential treatment, the selective application of formal rewards and punishments to inmates for money, the sale of paroles or other types of releases, and the use of state resources or property for one's own personal gain.

Malfeasance refers to direct misconduct by a staff member, as opposed to the improper use of legitimate authority. Corrupt practices in this category encompass primarily criminal acts, including theft, embezzlement, trafficking in contraband, and extortion.

Nonfeasance refers to the failure to live up to one's responsibilities or the omission of an act for which one is responsible. The two types of corrupt practices in this area are selectively ignoring inmate violations of institutional or organizations rules and the failure to report or deter other employees who are involved in corrupt behavior.

Factors Associated with Corruption

Two factors influence the degree of corruption experienced by a particular governmental agency. These are: (1) the opportunities for corruption, and (2) the level of incentives to make use of those opportunities. Opportunities for corruption arise from the discretionary authority given by the legislature to correctional officials. Punishment, in the form of withdrawal of privileges, transfers, or various forms of deprivation, are used to control inmates. The incentives for employees to engage in corruption may result from structural, organization, individual, or personal factors. Friendships with inmates, reciprocal relationships, and defaults undermine the formal control structure of the prison. The type and quality of staff may also affect prison corruption.

The Role of Opportunities

Three external forces influence prison systems and directly affect the incentives and opportunities for corruption. One is the continuing trend to incarcerate criminals. This led to unprecedented levels of crowding in state and federal prison systems. Second, career criminals are receiving longer sentences as the public sentiment toward punishment continues to harden. Third, citizen attitudes toward the treatment of prisoners have led to a toughening of programs directed at prison inmates.

Individuals sentenced to prison are subjected to various levels of deprivations, commonly referred to as "pains of imprisonment," which affect both the physical and psychological states of the individuals. Sykes defined these pains of imprisonment as the deprivation of liberty, goods and services, heterosexual relations, autonomy, and security. One of the techniques inmates use to soften the psychological and physical impact is the corruption of correctional employees as a means of neutralizing or improving their conditions of confinement.

Incentives for Corruption

A major incentive for corrupt practices results from defects in prison organization's control structure. The prison is essentially a coercive power. However, correctional employees, particularly line staff, find there are limits to the degree of compliance achieved through the use of coercive power. In order to do the job successfully, coercive power must be supplemented with informal exchange relations with inmates.

According to Sykes, three factors are responsible for undermining the formal control structure of the prison: (1) friendships with inmates, (2) reciprocal relationships, and (3) defaults. Each of these factors develops at the line-staff level as a function of long-term and close working associations between guard and inmate in a close setting. Corruption through friendship evolves from the close contact that prisoners and guards share in their daily interactions. Corruption through reciprocity occurs as an indirect consequence of the exchange relations that develop between inmates and staff. Corruption through default occurs when staff members begin to rely on inmates to assist them with their duties.

Cloward points out how defects in the prison organizations's control apparatus lead staff members to develop informal means of control. Material accommodations occur when staff provide certain inmates with access to forbidden goods and services or contraband in return for their cooperation. Power accommodations occur when selected inmates are provided with access to restricted information, such as the date and time of an impending shakedown. Status accommodations result when staff provide special deference to certain inmates. The cumulative effect of these accommodations may predispose certain correctional employees to take advantage of their situation and attempt to materially benefit from their working relationships with inmates, staff and contractors. The quality of employees hired provides another factor for corruption as well as an incentive for corruption due to the impact of politics.

Controlling Corruption

Corruption is a regular and traditional feature of governmental processes. While corruption can probably never be completely eliminated, there are certain steps that may be implemented to help control or minimize the problem. The first step in dealing with the problem of corruption is to develop and enforce a strict, zero-tolerance policy on corruption and implement and communicate a strong and forceful anti-corruption policy. This policy should define specifically what the agency means by corruption as well as specify the penalties associated with such practices.

Second, the correctional agency should develop a proactive mechanism to detect and investigate corrupt practices. This includes the establishment of an internal affairs unit and processes that encourage employees, inmates, and civilians to report allegations of staff misconduct. Third, the correctional administration needs to be open to improvement in management practices.

Another management enhancement practice would be to upgrade employee selection procedures to include psychological testing and formal pre-service training designed to screen out questionable employees. In addition, simple police checks of an individual's background should be expanded to include in-depth background investigations of prospective employees. The working conditions of employees also should be improved to enhance the quality of correctional work. Improving wage scales, enlarging job responsibilities, and broadening employee participation in decisionmaking, as well as increasing efforts toward professionalism, all will help address the issue of staff commitment to the mission of the agency.

A fourth and final recommendation addresses the political environment of prisons. By requiring merit selection and promotion of employees, a correctional administrator reduces the impact of political interference in the operation of the agency.

Conclusion

Controlling corruption requires a commitment by correctional administrators to provide leadership in setting high standards of ethical conduct, communicating and upholding standards of ethical behavior, and holding people accountable for their actions. Opportunities for corruption must be identified and addressed, and the risks taken by persons predisposed to misconduct must be increased. To upgrade and improve the prison in a democracy, we must make sure that the prison be opened to the public and its workings exposed to citizens.

Chapter 16

Ethics and Prison: Selected Issues

John T. Whitehead

Key Concepts

discrimination   privatization
elderly offenders   treatment
prison composition   victimization
prison conditions

Prison Composition

Only about 27 percent of persons incarcerated are admitted to prison for violent offenses. The majority of people sent to prison are neither violent nor career criminals. At the state level, however, six out of 10 prisoners are serving sentences for burglary or a violent offense. The debate about who should go to prison is influenced by politics that fail to consider all of the information. Critics of prisons overemphasize the composition; proponents oversell the alleged benefits.

Discrimination in Sentencing

The problem of racial discrimination is a pressing problem in corrections in the United States. The overrepresentation of African Americans in prison is a pervasive problem spanning more than 50 years. Although African Americans comprise about 12 percent of the overall U.S. population, they compose about 34 percent of the prison population. The drug laws that target crack cocaine are perceived by many simply to enhance the racial disparity in prison. This is a contentious subject that requires more research on the systemic effects of drug law enforcement in our culture.

Prison Conditions

The popular sentiment toward prison conditions calls for a tough prison system without television, recreation facilities, or athletic equipment. Some proponents argue for an increased workload for inmates to serve as punishment. However, there are some voices that believe that prison is already a painful punishment as it is. The deprivation of freedom, autonomy, possessions, security, and heterosexual contact should serve as ample punishment.

Treatment Programs

Rehabilitation has been routinely provided throughout the U.S. prison system. However, many conservatives simply want to provide punishment to the offenders and nothing else. Most prisoners are in dire need of some basic services, such as education. Many have alcohol or other drug problems. Some have psychological problems as well. Services to offenders can reduce recidivism when the inmate is released.

Safety in Prison

Victimization occurs within the prison institution. An inmate can be physically or sexually assaulted by another inmate or a guard. Studies differ in actual percentages reported. The ethical mandate here is to make all prisons safe and lawful— even the so-called "undeserving" should have this minimal guarantee.

Elderly Prisoners

Given the changes in sentencing in the past several years, it is likely that prison officials will see increasingly large numbers of prisoners in their sixties, seventies, and eighties. As the prisoners become elderly, many of them will be of no danger to society. The costs of keeping elderly persons incarcerated may become overwhelming.

Women in Prison

Women compose a small proportion of the incarcerated population of the United States. There are fewer women's prisons with fewer treatment programs. Moreover, the discipline women prisoners receive can be authoritarian. The ethical question here addresses the gender inequality that overlaps into prison.

Privatization

Generally, privatization of prisons is argued from an economic perspective. Competition should make private prisons more efficient, accountable, and effective. The ethical problem here involves whether it is appropriate for the government to relinquish control of prisoners to private business. Another related ethical problem includes whether businesses should make a profit at the expense of human suffering. The responsibilities of the private business to the inmates need to be very clear.

Chapter 17
Crime and Justice Myths

Egan Green

Key Concepts

deterrence

"Friend of a Friend"

"get tough" policies

juvenile superpredator

myth

three-strikes laws

war on drugs

Introduction

It is often the case that criminal justice policies are influenced by public opinion. It is a concern that crime myths, whether stereotypical or intentionally created, affect crime control policy.

The Nature of Myths

Myths have historically served a number of purposes including perpetuating a culture's ideals and protecting valued behaviors from outsider influence. They may be read or heard as stories of events or characters, but whatever the mode, they transmit values and accepted codes of behavior. Because myths are passed to consumers who are typically in agreement with the expressed values, their authenticity is seldom questioned. Myths allow differences in groups of people to be qualitative differentiations that dehumanize the group painted as inferior by the myth. Myths may raise an often fictional need for creating the criminals, yet they may also arouse belief in a need for more controls on existing criminals. Either way, people labeled as criminals become the "them" our society who pay the price.

The Media and Crime Myths

News networks are under tremendous pressure to report an event before the competition does so. Crime events are often used to lure viewers. Research also reveals a tendency among local news programs in large television markets to treat juvenile crime differently than adult crime. Juvenile crime is more likely to receive coverage that depicts it as occurring more often than it proportionally occurs. Other researchers have found evidence to support the notion that local television news is a source of information about, and therefore understanding of, criminal justice interactions. Popular media sources such as movies and television also present distorted images of crime as well as police, courts, and corrections work. Some media sources blur the line between popular media and news media by showing atypical depictions of illegal criminal justice events as standard practice.

Public perception of crime is likely to be shaped by all of these types of media influences. This means the public may be more likely to believe stereotypes of a failing criminal justice system that is hampered by the defendant protections as well as media-fed images of typical offenders, crime fighters, and victims. Such images often do not agree with actual crime facts.

Government, Politics, and Crime Myths

While society should be able to rely on the government and official crime facts and statistics to correct the course of crime myths, the unfortunate truth is that they are too often contributors to such images. Politicians often play on public fear of crime as a problem to be addressed. The public's fear of crime was an easy issue to address with answers such as greater enforcement and more severe punishment. In addition, to achieve the goal of creating a need for larger law enforcement budgets while still appearing successful, crime rates have been manipulated to present some problems as being solved while new ones are rising.

The General Public and Crime Myths

Bohm notes the different ways the general public contributes to crime myths as: (1) overgeneralizing personal experiences, (2) relying on inaccurate communication, (3) relying on atypical information, and (4) a lack of consciousness. Members of society often generalize their own experiences with crime or the criminal justice system as typical of everyday functioning of crime processing. People who have not had many direct dealings with crime and its consequences are often left to rely on the communications of those acquaintances who have. This lack of consciousness is the general public's failure to recognize, understand, or even know about many types of crime.

Myths About Crime

As is evident from the discussion of the news media's depiction of crime, street crime grabs headlines in part because of the public's fear of crime. This leads to the public's consensus to implement policies that focus on limiting this street crime. In turn, there is a severe discrepancy in law enforcement between street crime and corporate crime.

The myth that is perhaps the most persistent is that crime in the United States is rising, particularly violent crime. While crime rates in the United States are higher than in other industrialized nations, official crime rates indicate that while crime rates have fluctuated, overall reported violent crime incidents and rates were lower in 2005 than in 1986.

Myths About Criminals

An understanding of law creation and enforcement indicates that society has some firmly held ideas about who the law should control. The people who frighten most of society feel the brunt of law-creation movements and law-enforcement crack-downs. After increases in juvenile crime during the late 1980s and early 1990s, pre-dictions of juvenile superpredators started making their way into media and political discussions. A report by the Office of Juvenile Justice and Delinquency Prevention (1999) showed that juvenile violent crime rose slightly in the early 1990s, but came back to typical levels and even dropped by the late 1990s. The report also con-cluded that the rise in serious juvenile crime in the early 1990s was comparable to a similar trend that had occurred with previous generation of juveniles. There was no juvenile superpredator. Another crime myth is that violent crime is usually committed by strangers. However, stranger-committed crime is not as common as violence between family members and acquaintances. Nevertheless, the fear of being attacked by a stranger and media portrayals that reinforce this fear serve to further distort society's image of criminals.

Myths About Crime Control

Crime control policies continue to revolve around the idea of deterrence. The rational choice explanation fathered by Cesare Beccaria assumes that potential criminals will be deterred from committing crime if the likelihood of being caught is too high, or if the punishment for the offense is severe enough to outweigh the gain from committing the crime. Research shows that the United States is already implementing some of the most severe sanctions for crime in the world. The United States is acting on the principle of deterrence, and statistics indicate that it is not working to alleviate crime.

Crime Control Policy: Where Research and Politics Collide

With myths about criminals and crime in place, and a society susceptible to their placement, the public is looking for solutions. "Get tough" measures, three-strikes laws, and the war on drugs are examples of how myth can control crime control policy.

Conclusion

Media outlets, politicians, and the government all contribute to the public's perception of crime. These perceptions include the societal label of what behaviors are considered to be crime and who bears the title "criminal." Myths about crime end up harming all of society. Obviously, the public feels more fear of crime when fed a stream of images showing the threat coming from particular segments of society. Yet, the wrongly convicted and harmless offenders who have to serve severe sentences pay the highest price.

Chapter 18
The Ford Pinto Case and Beyond:
Assessing Blame

Francis T. Cullen, William J. Maakestad, Gray Cavender & Michael L. Benson

Key Concepts

    corporate misconduct
    political ethics
    white-collar crime

Introduction

Many citizens have become increasingly aware of the enormous costs incurred by white-collar crime, and that the rich and powerful can exact these harms with relative impunity. The matter has become one of not merely preventing victimization but also of confronting why crime allows "the rich to get richer and the poor to get prison." Public awareness of white-collar crime has reached the point at which the concept has become part of the common vernacular. In this social climate, the behavior of big business has taken on a new meaning. The world of big business was seen to suffer. For example, the case against Ford Motor Company brought by the State of Indiana was a manifestation of the broad movement against white-collar crime—and, in particular, against corporate crime.

Assessing Blame

The deaths of three girls in an automobile accident on August 10, 1978, in Indiana initiated a crusade against the Ford Motor Company. Ford Motor Company allegedly produced a vehicle, the Pinto, that was considered a lethal hazard because of the placement of the gas tank. The tank was highly susceptible to puncture during a rear-end collision; it would experience considerable fuel leakage and produce fires when hit even at low speeds. There was evidence that Ford was fully aware of this problem in the initial stages of production but chose not to fix the Pinto's defect because it was not cost-efficient.

In light of the facts surrounding the accident, coupled with a revision in Indiana's criminal code, the Indiana State's Attorney decided to charge Ford with a criminal offense: reckless homicide. The State's Attorney convened a grand jury to consider an indictment under the reckless homicide statute. After entertaining testimony from both Ford officials and safety experts who had previously served as witnesses in civil cases against Ford, the grand jury unanimously returned indictments against Ford Motor Company for three counts of reckless homicide. Ford's handling of the Pinto situation subsequently came to symbolize what was wrong with corporate America.

The Trial

With the potential costs of a prosecution running high, Ford Motor Company attempted to see that the case would never come before a jury. The result of Ford's efforts was a motion that argued that the criminal indictment should be dismissed on both conceptual and constitutional grounds. Ford contended that the reckless homicide statute could not be applied to corporate entities. They also asserted that the use of the word "person" in other places in the criminal code clearly is not meant to apply to corporations. Conceptual consistency would thus preclude corporations from being charged with violent offenses such as reckless homicide. Ford's constitutional defense hinged on the fact that the National Traffic and Motor Vehicle Safety Act had already created a federal apparatus to supervise the automobile industry. The second, more serious, constitutional matter raised by Ford's lawyers involved the ex post facto provision of both the Indiana and United States Constitutions.

The prosecution was able to meet both the conceptual and constitutional defenses proposed by Ford. They argued that a person, as defined by Indiana code, was "a human being, corporation, partnership, unincorporated association, or governmental entity." Additionally, the prosecution noted that the Indiana criminal code explicitly read that a corporation may be prosecuted for an offense. There was no conceptual inconsistency in the code. With regard to the constitutional issues, the prosecution asserted that the federal agency was not intended to deprive states of their police power. Likewise, the ex post facto defense was faulty given Ford's interpretation of when its offense occurred. The prosecution maintained that the defendant's omissions in regard to its obligation to either repair the 1973 Pinto or warn the owners of the car's hazards were important elements of the offense.

The judge ruled that Ford could not be charged for recklessly designing and manufacturing the Pinto. Instead, Ford was allegedly reckless in repairing the vehicle. Ford could be charged with failure to repair. The case was now ready to go to trial.

The trial was moved to another locality because it was doubtful that Ford would receive an impartial hearing in the locality where the crash had occurred. Ford initially won some important rulings, including the restriction of the gruesome photos of the victims of the crash. The judge also agreed with Ford and barred nearly all materials that predated the manufacture year of the specific Pinto in question (1973). This meant that any safety tests conducted on the Pinto by Ford or the government would be suppressed.

The prosecution was limited to two major lines of argument. First, it called in auto safety experts, including a former Ford executive who testified that the fuel tank on the Pinto was placed in a potentially lethal position. Second, the prosecution relied upon eyewitnesses to prove that the Pinto exploded despite being hit at a relatively low speed. The Ford defense team had two witnesses who testified that one of the victims in the crash had stated that the car was stopped on the highway. If so, the speed at impact would have been more than 50 miles per hour, a collision that no small car could have withstood. The defense also reminded jurors that Ford had voluntarily agreed to recall the Pinto two months before this particular accident. Ford argued that they had done everything feasible to warn Pinto owners; it certainly had not been reckless in this duty.

After days of deliberation, the jurors returned their verdict: not guilty. While Ford's prosecution was not devoid of legal precedents, it was certainly the most poignant example of a corporation being brought within the reach of the criminal law for allegedly perpetrating violence against innocent citizens.

Chapter 19
Ethics and Criminal Justice Research
Belinda R. McCarthy & Robin J. King

Key Concepts

codes of ethics
coercing participation
confidentiality
privacy

randomization
self-determination
willingness to participate

Problems Involving Work with Human Subjects

Stuart Cook (1976) lists the following ethical considerations surrounding research with human subjects:

1. Involving people in research without their knowledge.

2. Coercing people to participate.

3. Withholding from the participant the true nature of the research.

4. Deceiving the research participant.

5. Leading the research participant to commit acts that diminish their self-respect.

6. Violating the right to self-determination: research on behavior control and character change.

7. Exposing the research participant to physical or mental stress.

8. Invading the privacy of the research participant.

9. Withholding benefits from participants in control groups.

10. Failing to treat research participants fairly and to show them respect.

Balancing Scientific and Ethical Concerns

Cook (1976) identifies the potential benefits of a research project:

1. Advances in scientific theory that contribute to a general understanding of human behavior.

2. Advances in knowledge of practical value to society.

3. Gains for the research participant.

The potential cost to subjects are considerable, and it is often difficult for the researcher to be objective in assessing the issues. For this reason, many professional associations have established guidelines and procedures for ethical research conduct. The professional is honor-bound to follow these guidelines.

Ethical/Political Considerations

Applied social research that examines the effectiveness of social policies and programs carries additional ethical responsibilities. Sometimes research results conflict with cherished beliefs. Researchers can expect findings such as these to meet with considerable resistance. Often the truth is very complicated. Researchers who are employed by an organization for which the research is being conducted face special problems because of the lack of freedom to pick and choose their topics. In addition, researchers may be directly told to conceal or falsify results or may be encouraged to design their research with an eye toward the desired results of the company or organization. Such research influences the course of human events in a real fashion—often work, education, future opportunities, and deeply held values and beliefs are affected by the outcomes.

The Purity of Scientific Research

The ideal of scientific inquiry is the pure, objective examination of the empirical world, untainted by personal prejudice. However, research is carried out by human beings who have a variety of motivations for undertaking the research they do. The availability of grants in a particular field may also encourage researchers to direct their attention to these areas. The need for university faculty to publish and establish a name for themselves in a particular area may encourage them to seek "hot" topics for their research or to identify an extremely narrow research focus in which they become identified as an expert. While none of these practices involves violations of ethical conduct, they should remind us that actions justified in the name of scientific inquiry may be motivated by factors far less "pure" than the objective they serve.

Chapter 20

The Canary's Song:
Guantanamo and the War on Terrorism

John P. Crank & Patricia Gregor

Key Concepts

contested concept   *mens rea*
freedom fighter   terrorism
Guantanamo Bay prison camp   terrorist
habeas corpus

Introduction

The U.S. prison camp at Guantanamo Bay in Cuba is at the nexus of all the controversies that are associated with the war on terrorism. Ethically it is a watershed event: Advocates of legal fair play contend that Guantanamo is in violation of all U.S. and international notions of justice, while supporters of Guantanamo detainment argue that the war on terrorism is so important that the way it is carried out should be outside the bounds of law.

Problems with Defining Terrorism

It is important to note that this is a war on a concept "terrorism," not on a category of people "terrorists." Guantanamo is argued in this chapter as a controversy precisely because terrorism is a contested concept. Rush gives a four-part definition of terrorism. First, terrorism is the calculated use of violence to obtain political goals through instilling fear, intimidation, or coercion. Second, it is the climate of fear or intimidation created by means of threats or violent actions, causing sustained fear for personal safety, in order to achieve social or political goals. Third, it is an organized pattern of violent behavior designed to influence government policy or intimidate the population. Fourth, it is violent criminal behavior designed primarily to generate fear in the community for political purposes. This definition focuses on motive rather than behavior. However, this has little to do with how the government defines terrorism.

It is in the criminal intent, the *mens rea*, that we determine if the event is terrorist. The U.S. Code refers to international terrorism as activities that (a) involve violent acts or acts dangerous to human life that are a violation of the criminal laws of the United States or of any state, or that would be a criminal violation if committed within the jurisdiction of the United States or of any state. Domestic terrorism refers to activities that involve acts dangerous to human life that are a violation of the criminal laws of the United States or of any state; and appear to be intended. The PATRIOT Act added that domestic terrorism (b) appears to be intended to intimidate or coerce a civilian population; to influence the policy of a government by intimidation or coercion; or to affect the conduct of a government by mass destruction, assassination, or kidnaping.

These definitions do not provide insight into the way in which the United States responded to the terrorist attacks of September 11, 2001. Law enforcement is adequate if the source of the threat can be isolated to particular individuals. However, once state-supported players become involved, a more robust response involving the U.S. military is required. We shift the working definition of terrorism from a body of articulable U.S. law, as determined by the state legislature and carried out by the judiciary, to the executive branch.

In 1996, an Antiterrorism and Effective Death Penalty Act gave the Secretary of State the discretion to decide who was on the government's terrorism list. Consequences apply to members of these groups. For example, contributing money to these groups, even for humanitarian reasons, is a crime. Members of these groups are also barred from entering the United States and can be deported if they are already in the country. Third, banks can freeze the funds of these organizations and their agents. A watch list of five million individuals is held by the United States. Citizens of individual "terrorist" nation-states are also on the watch list. These states are Cuba, Iran, Iraq, Lybia, Syria, Sudan, and the Democratic People's Republic of Korea. The National Security Entry-Exit Registration System was implemented in order to track individuals in the United States who hail from these countries. What we see in the "working definition of terrorism" is that it is categorical, that is, it is based on lists of known persons, terrorist organizations, and nation-states.

Terrorism as a Contested Concept

"One man's terrorist is another man's freedom fighter." This statement has two elements. First, is the way in which the label "terrorism" changes over time. The second element is that individuals who are seen as heroes or "freedom fighters" by one group are seen as terrorists by another. This means the definition of terrorism is largely one of political utility. In other words, who is a terrorist and who is a freedom fighter depends not only on time and place but also on which side of a conflict someone is on. The central problem with a contested definition of terrorism is that the working definition is created and acted out in a political environment, influenced by emotions, ideology, and religious predispositions of those in power.

"War Versus Crime" as a Contested Area

This issue asks whether individuals should be treated as criminals, which would mean they have access to the U.S. court system. Soros argues that the 9/11 attacks should have been treated as a crime against humanity. However, Turk argues there are fundamental limitations to individualized justice as provided by the U.S. justice system.

Guantanamo

Guantanamo stands at the nexus of the war/crime controversy. Secretary Rumsfeld undertook the establishment of a high-security detention facility at the U.S. Naval Base in Guantanamo. Guantanamo was designed to take about 100 prisoners initially and hold up to 2,000, it was staffed by a Joint Task force of 160 persons, and comprised around 1,000 soldiers from various bases in the United States. Prisoners were housed in cells that measured six feet wide and eight feet long and high. In 2002, Camp X-ray prisoners were moved to Camp Delta. The principal reason for holding detainees at Guantanamo is that it is not located on U.S. soil. Prisoners are held at Guantanamo for two reasons. First, the value of information gained during interrogation for antiterrorism purposes is likely to deteriorate fairly quickly in time. Second, there is a fear of overlooking a very dangerous terrorist who might commit or has committed grave acts against the country.

Military Tribunals For Guantanamo Detainees

President Bush authorized the creation of military tribunals in 2001 in order to try noncitizens on charges of terrorism. In 2002, the rules for tribunals were revised. Conviction and sentencing would require a two-thirds majority, and there would be three to seven panelists participating who would be military officers. The guidelines were revised again in 2004 to give lawyers more information about whether the government will eavesdrop on conversations between detainees and their council, although the government continues to retain the right to eavesdrop. If persons are found guilty in the tribunals, the Executive will be accused internationally and by many groups in the United States of kangaroo justice against 9/11 detainees. If detainees are found innocent, the Executive will be accused of overreaching, and its justification for Guantanamo will be undercut.

Redefining Justice in the War on Terrorism

The war on terror has permitted the redefinition of the relationship between crime control and due process. The war on terror has changed this relationship. In the new model, crime control issues are prioritized over due process and crime control issues are reframed as security issues. Only after security issues are resolved are due process concerns considered.

The Song of the Canary

Guantanamo is in many ways the canary in the coal mine. What happens in Guantanamo harkens to wider justice trends toward a reframed notion of crime control as security, which is prioritized over due process. "If you want a definition of this place, you don't have a right to have rights," said a detainee. The problem is that we do not have in place a legal mechanism to determine if persons are who the government claims they are. The canary song, for both sides in the contested war on terrorism and as acted out at Guantanamo, is filled with suffering and injustice. This is a paradox. In the way we conduct the war on terrorism today, the more one side seeks to re-establish its sense of justice, the greater the injustice is to the other side.

Terrorism, Liberty, and Security

We return to the central problem with a war on terrorism. It is a war on a contested concept. The central question is between security and liberty, which can be framed in terms of the importance of utilitarian good ends versus the rightness of fair play. Changes were brought about due to 9/11. First, there was a retexting of crime control in terms of the language of international security, whether or not security was international or internal to the United States. Second, there was a broadening of administrative control of suspects by the Executive in the name of security, in lieu of due process or habeas corpus. Habeas corpus is the right to appeal the assertion of the holding authority to some court to have their case reviewed. The executive branch has taken a utilitarian view of the war and argues for a forceful response to terrorism.

Chapter 21
Criminal Justice:
An Ethic for the Future

Michael C. Braswell

Key Concepts

mindfulness
order-keeping
peacemaking

The Need for Mindfulness

If we are to develop an ethic for the future of criminal justice, we need to become more mindful and conscious of ethical truths concerning justice that are found in the present. We are all connected: parents to children, guards to prisoners, and offenders to victims. Although we are all bound together in society, we may still find it necessary to remove an offender from our midst. However, we must ensure that offenders are treated humanely on ethical and moral grounds. The promise of the future connects us in the knowledge that most offenders, especially with current overcrowding problems, will eventually return to our communities. Becoming more mindful can allow us, as individuals and communities, to take greater care in seeing and responding more meaningfully to the connections that bind us together in relationships.

Order-Keeping and Peacekeeping

Our search for justice can become subverted to a search for order only. We imagine that if we can just do things more efficiently, crime and justice problems can eventually be solved, or at least reduced to an insignificant level. However, this belief misses the larger truth. While keeping order is important, keeping peace is more than that.

Peacekeeping represents a larger vision for the individual and the community. If we are to contribute to a more just society, we must not simply think, talk, or write about peacekeeping and peacemaking, but personally struggle to be increasingly peaceful. Peacekeeping, in fact, becomes a practice of peacemaking.

Some Suggestions for Criminal Justice

If we are to look to the future of criminal justice with some measure of hope rather than a growing sense of cynicism, we must seek out fresh possibilities rather than defend traditional certainties. It seems more important than ever for us to look past our individual and agency interests into the larger community of which we are a part. Three areas in which this "wholesight" may be better employed within the criminal justice system are: (1) law and justice, (2) policing, and (3) corrections.

Law and Justice

The way we define laws and the way our justice system enforces them can enhance or diminish our opportunities for more peaceful and orderly communities. Additionally, issues of law and justice must be struggled with on a personal level. For example, it seems that many persons have come to believe that a legal act and a moral act are essentially the same. In life or in criminal court, when we do get caught, our plea is for mercy. Whether dealing with minor greed or major fraud, when we are the victims, we are inclined to want retribution, yet when we are the offender, we want mercy.

Policing

With more diversity within the ranks of policing, the opportunity exists for a greater openness in redefining police roles and functions. A clearer focus concerning the need for police officers to possess meaningful communication and interpersonal skills should become apparent. The more mindful police are with the ethic of care as translated through effective communication and interpersonal skills, the less likely they are to have to "get tough" with the people with whom they come in contact. Given the discretion and immediacy of response utilized by police officers in the community setting, there is perhaps no other criminal justice professional who is as connected to the community and who has as great an opportunity to contribute to the community's sense of care and well-being.

Corrections

Corrections directly addresses the "least of the community"—the "two-time losers," the nuisance factor, the disenfranchised, and the violent. We need to develop and more clearly articulate a treatment ethic that is restorative in nature and that more honestly addresses the community's sense of duty to itself. Because offenders are perceived as the least useful to the community, the larger community often feels, retributively, that such persons are deserving of the least care.

Justice as a Way Rather than a Destination

We need an ethic for the future that will empower us to act on an enlarged vision of what justice is about, a vision that will include the community of which we are all a part—the best of us and the worst of us—the best in *each* of us and the worst in *each* of us.

Justice as a way of service requires more than just the passionate zeal of the visionary, it also requires the mindfulness of quiet compassion. Only peace has the potential to remain calm and resolute even in the midst of suffering, which is an experience that connects each of us to the other in the community. Peace comes from the inside out. People at peace with themselves create peaceful organizations that can then become instruments for peacemaking in the larger community.